TRUST ME

(you couldn't make this up)

TRUST ME

(you couldn't make this up)

Scott Sturgess

Published in Australia by Sid Harta Books & Print Pty Ltd,
ABN: 34632585293
23 Stirling Crescent, Glen Waverley, Victoria 3150 Australia
Telephone: +61 3 9560 9920
E-mail: author@sidharta.com.au

First published in Australia 2021
This edition published 2021

Cover design, typesetting: WorkingType (www.workingtype.com.au)

Scott Sturgess
Trust Me
ISBN: 978-1-925707-67-0
pp208

ABOUT THE AUTHOR

Scott Sturgess has a short attention span. After graduating in Veterinary Science from the University of Queensland in 1968, he was conscripted into the army and served in Vietnam in 1970. He subsequently spent eight years in private veterinary practice and five more farming and wasting money on racehorses.

A need for his family to eat saw him working as a government vet in western and far-north Queensland, during which time he was sent to Central America to work briefly with the United States Department of Agriculture. Three years in Landcare and Catchment Management then preceded a stint as a policy advisor in Queensland's short-lived Borbidge government. Work in the United Kingdom's Meat Hygiene Service followed electoral defeat, but he came back to Oz in 2000 as Manager of Industry Development in Western Australia's Southern Rangelands. He then returned to England for a while when Foot and Mouth Disease broke out.

Back in Australia he bought a Darling Downs farm and worked as a Meatworks Contract Vet. An early 2008 visit to Antarctica was a revelation. Noting that penguins, if given the choice, would rather stay where they were than move to the Sunshine Coast, he pondered the possibility of settling down in the one spot. This led to the purchase of a lychee farm twelve years ago and he and his relieved wife, Flora, are still there in 2021.

PREFACE

This is not designed to be my life story; there is nothing special about me. However, I have had a lot of interesting and amusing experiences and been told a lot of interesting and amusing stories. I believe they are worth recording. Every one involving me is true. I cannot totally vouch for the stories told to me but believe the majority are mostly true. There may be a couple which stretch the bounds of credibility. The reader can judge.

If I have included details which make you wonder where I got them from, the answer is probably Wikipedia.

CONTENTS

LOLOMA

I am the sixth and last child, all boys, of my generation of my family and when I started to write this, one of only two survivors. The three oldest brothers were long dead and the fourth had just died. It gives one pause to reflect on age and the passage of time. At 75, perhaps I should be grateful that there are still two of us left, although these days 75 is not considered all that old, unless you want life insurance—no stiff joints, firm muscles, unwrinkled skin, a good night's uninterrupted sleep, dietary indulgence and ... I had better stop because this is making me depressed.

It recently occurred to me that many of the normal day-to-day events and habits of my early life are so different from those of current times that it might be a good idea to document some of them for the benefit, if they ever read this, of my grandchildren, and even theirs. Things that did not rate a second thought in the 1950s would invoke shrieks of horror now. For example, my parents had a dairy farm in those days. Not that that should cause shrieks of horror, but some of their regular procedures might these days.

Lots of people had dairy farms back then. The governments in the early days of Queensland's, and I guess Australia's, settlement encouraged dairy farming as a way to open up the land and spread the population into the interior. It was a sad mistake in many cases because the decision makers, in their ignorance, assumed that Australian dairy farms would need to be only the same size as England's ones. Of course, England is beautiful and green 95 percent of the time whereas Australia's interior is brown and dry 95 percent of the time. The planners only had to get off their arses and go and have a look to see the difference, but that apparently never happened. Blocks of 160 acres far into the interior are a sad indictment of their incompetence and the 'Soldier Settlement' scheme after World War 1 was, in many cases, a total disaster.

Despite that, there were lots of dairy farms left and we had one, called 'Loloma'. Early milking was by hand, although by the time I came along milking was done by machine. Fortunately, I never had to help with the milking. We stopped dairying when I was five, but my oldest brothers had to work in the dairy before and after school.

These days the milk is collected into stainless steel refrigerated vats and picked up from the farms daily by refrigerated tankers. In the 1950s, things were a lot different. Milk was separated on farm into cream and skim milk. The milk was either fed to pigs or to calves which had been taken from their mothers. The cream was stored in cans inside what we called the cream dairy. It was a small building about three metres square, on a concrete base with wooden sides and gauze windows all round to permit free flow of air. Can you believe it would stay there, unrefrigerated, for two or three days before it was driven to town to the dairy cooperative by my father, older brother, or one of the dairy farming neighbours? My mother always claimed that cream needed to be sour to make the best butter and I guess two or three days out of the 'fridge' might do it! Much of the butter that was produced was sold to the United Kingdom, so I suppose the cream must have been pasteurised before the butter was made.

Our vehicle in the earliest days I can remember was a 1928 Buick. In about 1950, Dad bought an Austin A70 and the Buick was converted into a ute by the simple process of removing all of the roof, sides and back which kept the weather out. It functioned for many years and my second oldest brother, Max, who worked and lived on the farm at that time, would sometimes drive down to the Condamine River which flowed intermittently through the neighbour's property, to go fishing. One of my earliest memories is of an occasion when I wanted to accompany him but, no doubt, had been refused. I got into the back of the ute and hid under an old tarpaulin that was lying there. I cannot have been more than four years old and was worried that I might get into trouble or might accidentally come to harm, so I sat up, still covered by the tarp! I think I knew I would be seen. Let's face it, I would be pretty stupid, even at four, to think I would not be, but perhaps I thought my obvious enthusiasm would cause the adults to relent. It didn't. Mum and Max laughed a lot but I stayed home.

Another event which I clearly recall from around that time was the day I ran over the brown snake on my three-wheeler bike. We did not call them tricycles; they were three-wheelers. (Not being familiar with Latin or Greek roots at that time, I had no trouble reconciling with the concept of a three-wheeled bicycle!) I was hurtling up the road outside the house with the grim determination that only a four-year-old can muster when I saw the snake lying across my path. I must have registered it, but my brain cannot have progressed to the next logical step—avoidance—before I arrived and ran over the reptile about 30cm from its head. It swung back, either to escape or to bite me, but fortunately, if it did want to strike, it missed. My brother, Lester, was with me at the time and we rushed inside to tell the grown-ups, one of whom came out and killed the snake. Snakes were not protected in those days and even if they had been, they wouldn't have been near our house.

It was a red-letter day when Dad bought a new car and we were all highly impressed, not least because the Austin A70 had turning indicators. They consisted of two illuminated arms that folded down into the body frames between the front and back doors. At least I think there were two. Indicating left turns was not a high priority those days and even with the indicators many people signalled right turns with their hands extended. Interior switches for the lights were common by that time although there were still plenty of vehicles around that required the driver to stop and get out to switch on the tail lights. The switch was usually beside the back number plate. I recall a story about some acquaintance of ours who said he had driven on a mountain road so winding that he could reach out of the window and turn on the tail lights!

The house on our farm contained two bedrooms, a verandah on one side and a sleepout on the other. One never hears the term sleepout any more—it is basically a verandah with windows or essentially, a long, thin bedroom, usually for children, of which in those days there were often plenty. A short distance away was the shed. I did not find out for many years, but the shed had actually been the original house. My father had acquired the farm by assuming the debts of the previous owner, but it was pretty wild and covered with large areas of brigalow, belah and box trees. He cleared the trees by hand for a big enough area to build a house, then built the house before bringing Mum and one or two of my oldest brothers there to live. It was hardly a mansion but it was a house. It is hard for me to imagine the determination he must have had to do that. My father had worked for some time in the timber industry in the Sunshine Coast hinterland and it was there that he had acquired useful woodworking skills. Several years later, the house on a neighbouring farm burned down and a number of other neighbours got together and built a new one! According to my cousin who lives in that house now, more than eighty years later, Dad was the 'master builder' and oversaw the whole exercise. It's not a bad house. Imagine trying to do that today. I moved a house from Toowoomba onto a farm nearby early this century and the bureaucratic interference had to be seen to be believed. I shall write more about that later.

There used to be a small school, Greenswamp State School, a couple of miles back towards town from 'Loloma' and all of the brothers except me spent some time there, riding horses to and fro. The oldest three did all of their primary schooling there. They were not supposed to gallop the horses, but a local farmer who lived nearby was quoted as having said, 'They arrived in a lather of sweat and left in a cloud of dust.'

In the late 1940s the school shut down and Mum taught my brothers, Jack and Lester, by correspondence. After a year of that I was old enough to start and she bailed up, refusing to teach three kids. Hard to blame her really, so Dad bought a house in Chinchilla. It was fortuitous that Max, who had been away chasing his future wife, caught her about then, married her and brought her back to live, and Max to work, on the farm.

Greenswamp School was named after Greenswamp Lagoon, which was a large lagoon on a nearby property. It was perhaps 400m long and 150m wide. There was no town swimming pool in Chinchilla at that time and Greenswamp Lagoon was the local substitute, albeit about five or six miles away. It was a regular venue for carnivals and boasted a 'diving tower' about three metres square with a springboard maybe 3m above the water and a platform for the especially brave or foolhardy another 3m above that. This was built on the edge of the water so at that point at least it must have been quite deep. The lagoon was about 300 or 400m from Charleys Creek, a tributary of the Condamine River and I can only assume it had always been there. Perhaps it filled when the creek flooded and a local gully would have run into it. It remained a significant waterhole for most of my childhood and youth but then dried up. It is a mystery because clearing and cultivating the land is supposed to increase runoff and it happened long before those who are inclined to blame global warming for such incidents, had ever heard the phrase.

As well as the diving tower, the lagoon also boasted a smaller diving board 20 or 30m away, where we kids would all line up and take turns to dive, jump, or whatever, to the cheers of onlookers. The water was perhaps 1.5m deep under the end of the board. People do some stupid things, and I am one such person. On one occasion I decided, for my trick, to hold my hands down by my side and just tip forward and enter the water head first. That worked perfectly, but after passing through the water, my head hit the ground beneath quite hard. I could easily have broken my neck and rendered myself quadriplegic. How brainless! Fortunately, we all drank lots of milk and had strong bones—I do not recall any of us ever having fractures.

* * *

SCHOOL

Moving into Chinchilla to go to school was a major event. We had carpet on the floor of the bedrooms and 240V electricity and were warned about the potentially fatal consequences if we poked wire into the power points. Why anybody in their right mind would even consider such a move was beyond me then and remains a mystery! On the farm we had a bank of 12 volt batteries powered by a petrol engine that required starting every night. It was monumentally inefficient and whenever an extra light was turned on, all of the ones already lit would go darker. It ingrained the habit I still possess of turning lights off when they are not needed.

The town house was made of fibrous cement. Lots of houses were made of 'fibro' in those days. It was cheap, easy to use and lasted well. It was much better than the stuff that masquerades as fibro these days, because it contained asbestos! How did we survive? I spent many years sleeping beside a depressed V-shaped fracture in the panel beside my bed, which I had caused fighting with my brother. It makes me laugh when I see the ridiculous extremes that are gone to when asbestos, usually fibro, is discovered on demolition or building sites. If I am going to get the dreaded mesothelioma, it is surely taking its time.

Living in a country town in Australia in the 1950s was a wonderful experience. I suppose there were wife-beaters, pedophiles and all manner of antisocial behaviour, but it must have been well hidden. Actually, there was one incident where a local mechanic named Albert was supposed to have committed some indecent act with a couple of thirteen-year-old boys. I'm not sure what the outcome was—the boys certainly did not seem to have been scarred by the experience, whatever it was. I later heard that when the offender appeared at work shortly after, someone shouted, 'Backs to the wall, boys, here comes Albert!' As far as I know, that was all the punishment he got.

(Albert had quite an exotic surname and that was not unusual in Chinchilla. Despite the fact that Australia's population was, and still is, considered essentially of British origin, there must have been immigrants from all over the world coming to Queensland in the early days. I am still amazed by the number of surnames that existed in Chinchilla in the 1950s that I have never seen since.

Cadzows from Scotland and Mutschs from England may not have been surprising, but Hohnke, Zeller and Petsch from Germany, Knudsen from Scandinavia and d'Anglaids from France existed alongside the Reuschels, Lebsanfts and Fraunfelters whose origins I have never been able to trace.)

Of course, there were a lot fewer people then, and there was not a media class which gleefully disseminated news of Albert's kind of behaviour to fill the space generated by the 24-hour news cycle, whatever that is, so our awareness was minimal. We kids certainly never felt threatened at any time, day or night. From the age of about thirteen I used to walk about 1.5km every Friday night to the Star picture theatre and walk home after the show finished at about 10pm. After cleaning my teeth with copious amounts of toothpaste, I would go into Mum and Dad's bedroom and kiss Mum goodnight, naively believing that she, a non-smoker, would not smell my breath!

The Catholics and Protestants divide was still a real thing in those days and the stupidity and persistence of that attitude remain a mystery to me. I used to walk past the Catholic School on my way to the State School and was encouraged by my fellow state schoolmates to scorn and deride the RCs and the nuns. I'm not sure why, but logic is not always front and centre with twelve-year-olds. Of course, when I got home from school, I played happily with Michael, my Catholic neighbour, and we had great games together, except once, when he nearly blinded me! Not deliberately, I hasten to say.

Chinchilla at that time had no town water system so Dad and Michael's father engaged a local resident to dig us wells. It was done by placing a concrete cylinder approximately 1.5m in diameter and perhaps a little longer, end on, on the ground. Then the well digger would dig out the earth inside the cylinder so it would gradually sink. When the top had reached ground level another cylinder would be added and this process would continue until water had been reached, from memory about 6 or 7m down. Ours was done first and Michael's back yard was, for a time, strewn with concrete cylinders which we utilised for various games. On one occasion I crept over the top and he emerged below and 'shot' up at me with his gun, a pointed piece of pine board. Unfortunately, he got me in the eye! Pain and drama! Fortunately, both my eye and our friendship survived and I enjoy his company even now, on the odd occasions I meet him at the racetrack.

Back in those days, not many country towns had sewerage. We had outside toilets—small, square, weatherboard buildings containing a seat over a metal can which would be removed and replaced by an empty one every week. We males were never allowed to urinate in the can because it might fill up too soon—a potential disaster! Current generations will probably be surprised to find that women and children used chamber pots to save having to go outside in the middle of the night, though I expect that a nocturnal trek would be necessary if anything more than a piddle was needed. Sewerage was introduced to Chinchilla many years later while I was at boarding school and it was a pleasant surprise to arrive home for holidays one time to find an indoor toilet had been installed.

A couple of years after coming to town, I learned to ride a bicycle. Brother Lester had one. I was too short to sit on the seat, but I could sit on the bar in front and would get out of bed early and go for a ride before the house woke up. Our roads were not bitumen; they were coated with a sort of white, crumbly gravel which was often present in lumps as big as a tennis ball. One morning I accidentally rode over one such lump and the front wheel shot sideways, dropping me on the ground. I landed quite heavily and lay for a while wondering if I had sustained any injury. When I got up, I was alarmed to find that my head was bleeding! At school I had often heard people talk of so and so who had split his head open. I never knew what that entailed but imagined a gaping hole through which pulsing brain could be viewed. I HAD SPLIT MY HEAD OPEN! Bravely struggling back onto the bike, I raced home as fast as my declining strength would allow and ran into the parents' bedroom shouting, 'Mum! Mum! I've split my head open!' Mum took a quick look and said, 'That's all right. Dab a bit of kerosene on it.' 'Kero' was mum's first response drug of choice. I was devastated by her heartlessness.

It's funny how expressions which people never queried have suddenly become politically incorrect. There used to be a school fundraising event to which people went along in the evening and played WOGS. It was a dice game where different numbers represented wings, legs, feelers, etcetera, of an unnamed insect. Back in those days a 'wog' was an insect, but sometimes it was also a germ. I can remember my mother once explaining that she had been sick recently and spent a few days in bed with some wog! Imagine the horror these days! The adultery would pale into insignificance next to the racism shrieks!

I did well at school and never used to cheat in exams, unlike a couple of my competitors at the top of the class. I don't know if it was because my great-grandfather was a convict and we all felt we had to compensate, although probably not, because I didn't even know about him until years later. But it might have influenced my parents because my brothers and I were all brought up to totally respect authority and the law. There was never any debate. Naturally, I believed that the majority of people behaved the same way that we did, other than hardened criminals, and it took years for me to realise how naïve I was.

There used to be a state-wide exam called the Scholarship Exam for all grade eight pupils at the end of the school year. The Lilley Medal was awarded to the boy or girl who came top of the state and naturally a great deal of prestige was attached to that. I was considered having a good chance of winning it, but unfortunately, I missed out. It may seem that we were a bit ambitious expecting a pupil from a small country school to top the state, but there was form. The previous year had seen a Chinchilla pupil win the medal and a local won again the year after me. It was all down to our remarkable teacher, Mrs Brown. The first day of grade eight, in Mrs Brown's class, we were all given definitions of various events or things that she considered relevant to our social studies course. We wrote them down. The next day, we were asked to write out explanations of the various subjects she had provided definitions for. I had a general idea, as did most of us, but that was not nearly enough. It soon became apparent that we were supposed to write out word perfectly the definitions she had given us the previous day. After spending an hour 'kept in' after school to revise our definitions, we made sure we got them right in future.

Despite her being such a high performer, Mrs Brown was only paid 80 percent of the salary that a male teacher got. Can you believe that? In those days, married women were not allowed to teach at all. There were plenty of single women teachers, but as soon as they married, they lost their jobs. Mrs Brown was only exempted from that rule because her husband was an invalid!

I started high school in Chinchilla at the same time that my father and a few of his friends started the Chinchilla picnic race club. There was a racecourse on the edge of town, but there had been no races for many years. I was hooked from day one and remain hooked! The picnics were different from the usual professional races in that the jockeys were amateurs and the horses had to be put in a paddock and just eat grass for several weeks before going into training for a short while, so theoretically at least, they all started training from the same state of fitness. We would hear tales of unscrupulous types who might creep out in the dead of night to give their horses a feed of oats, but I never heard of anyone being caught doing it. It was probably just sour grapes after a loss!

Dad and my brother, Max, used to train our horses and one year I was riding one of our mares, Miss Confidence, Dad's favourite, in her exercise. On this occasion, for some reason, we were in the showgrounds arena which was only about 400m in circumference. As the mare galloped, the exercise saddle started to slip back and roll inwards.

Attempting to correct it, I stamped down hard on my left foot and succeeded in rolling the saddle and myself straight over so I fell heavily on the hard ground. Miss Confidence galloped off into the yards where campdraft cattle were kept at show time, and a piece of loose wire just faintly scratched the skin of her hip as she went through a narrow gap. I just lay on the ground checking myself for broken bones and waiting for my father to arrive and sympathise with my plight. After quite a long wait, he did arrive, and said, 'You useless bastard, she might have knocked her hip down running through that gate!' He had expended all of his sympathy on the horse; there was none left for me!

I did merit the odd concession though. It probably seems a bit politically incorrect these days, but on my fourteenth birthday, I was given a rifle. It was a beautiful, fifteen-shot, semi-automatic .22 with a tube magazine which ran under the barrel. I still have trouble believing it was given to me. Frequently on weekends, I would get a lift out to the farm with Dad and go shooting while he worked. Sometimes a friend came with me but I often went alone. I rarely shot anything because there wasn't all that much to shoot, but one unlucky wallaby could keep me enthusiastic for weeks.

From quite an early age, we children all did some work on the farm. Tractors were becoming bigger and better and cultivation of land for crops was increasing. Of course, the land must first be cleared, so many tiresome weekends were spent picking up sticks so they would not either puncture tractor tyres or clog up ploughs. What a bugger of a job. From the age of about fourteen, my brother, Lester, and I also drove the tractors for ploughing, which does not sound too bad if you think about how it looks these days. Sixty years ago, we had no air-conditioned cabs and in fact not even a canopy. It was a great technological breakthrough for us when our older brother, Max, fitted a beach umbrella over the seat. Small tractors and small ploughs, and we had to stop regularly to grease them. There were no sealed bearings in those days, or not in our ploughs anyhow. Even a relatively small 20 or 30ha paddock seemed to take forever to get around and the pathetically narrow width that the discs disturbed meant that there were plenty of circuits to do!

Of course, the reward for all of this hard work came at harvest time. Once again, harvesting was a bit different then from what it is today. We had a small header which was pulled by the tractor. This machine cut the tops off the wheat stalks, threshed them, dropped the husks and stalks out the back and put the grain in a built-in bin. The grain bin held about ten bags of wheat and when it was full, the tractor was stopped and the grain was put in bags. The bin had two small, vertical sliding doors, each one above a hinged square frame to which a three-bushel bag would be attached. Once the bag was secured in position, the door would be raised and the grain rushed out. When it was done, the tractor driver would take off and the men who bagged the wheat would then sew up the bags. A three-bushel bag of wheat weighed 180lb, about 80kg, so they are not all that easy to manhandle, especially if you are only fourteen or fifteen years old. The problem was, that to fit 180lb of wheat in a bag, you had to fill it pretty full. That meant that when the bag was 90 per cent sewn, the wheat would be starting to squeeze out of the top. The only way to overcome this was to lift the bag up and drop it down a couple of times to settle the grain. Not all that easy for a kid, but I managed by bending my knees, clamping them onto the bag, then straightening up and dropping the bag. Child labour! We got paid £2 per day, or maybe it was one per day, two per weekend!

When I was almost sixteen, a bunch of my school-mates and I organised a party one Saturday night in the Presbyterian Church hall. This was a fairly big deal and I had arranged, informally, to go and collect my current 'girlfriend' and escort her to and from the event. This was revolutionary for me. Never had I engaged in such a public display of sentiment, but I was feeling pretty good about the whole idea. When the fateful Saturday arrived, Dad finished breakfast and indicated that we must get in the car and drive out to the farm because it was harvest time. I asked when we might get back and on hearing that it would be an hour or two after my scheduled girlfriend pickup, I explained my situation and said that I was not coming! Well! Sorry about that, Scott! That might have been the last time I ever did sew wheat bags, but I have never forgotten.

* * *

Tennis was very popular back in those days. All of the country schools had tennis courts, even the very small schools, and many of them had tournaments in the winter months. It seems there would be a tournament every second week, even at places where there was no town, just a school and nothing else. I was a handy player but no champion. I could usually win a few matches until I met one of the good players who would give me a thrashing, but it was always fun. On one occasion I was invited to accompany a good player, Ken, as his doubles partner to a tournament at a place called Hannaford. The usual partner was unavailable. I was to stay the weekend at Ken's parents' farm and we would drive to Hannaford in the family Holden ute, with Ken and I and another friend sitting in the back. There were no seatbelts in those days, even in the front, and certainly not in the back of a utility. The day worked out well. Ken won the singles and he and I won the doubles, but the trip home was something else. This was in the August school holidays and it can get pretty cold at that time of year. We lay down in the back of the ute for the one-hour trip home with a flimsy blanket to cover us. By the time we arrived, my legs were numb from the knees down! Not just cold—numb. We went inside and someone lit a kerosene heater to warm us up and I actually burnt myself by getting too close to the heat because my legs could not feel pain.

In my final year of school at Chinchilla, now called Year 10, but then called Junior, some friends lent me a horse and I played polocrosse. It was the most wonderful experience and even though I was only fifteen, I was fairly handy. There were no junior teams back then so I played with the adults. Towards the end of the season a new club called Tansey, in the Burnett area, decided to hold a one-day carnival. Polocrosse carnivals were usually two days but there were not a lot of clubs in that region at that time, so there would not have been enough competitors to justify two days. Chinchilla sent two teams and we were expected to win because we were much more experienced at that time than the Burnett teams. I played in number two position in Chinchilla's number one team which, to my serious disappointment, was beaten by Chinchilla Two in the final. However, I won the trophy as the best Number Two player, the only time I ever won an individual sporting trophy in my whole life! I took it home a bit surprised but very pleased and shortly afterwards it was engraved:

Best Number Two
Tansey Polocrosse Carnival 1961
Scott Sturgess.

My father was brought up in a very tough school and he was a very tough man. In all my life he never ever said to me, 'Well done, son,' but I think it was he who got the engraving done.

That is pretty much the end of my Chinchilla story as I went to boarding school in sub-senior (Year 11) and only ever came home for holidays from then on, but there is one last thing that bears mentioning. On our farm, and all of the neighbouring farms I ever visited in that area, there were dozens of what we called 'army bolts', which some others called 'Yankee bolts'. They were 3/8in galvanised bolts, about 2ft (60cm) long, each with a rounded head and a big washer and nut on the end. People used them for a vast number of purposes, either whole, cut up, or bent into useful shapes. They were so ubiquitous that I never wondered where they came from; they were just there. It turns out that during World War II there was a United States army munitions camp at Columboola, on the railway line between Chinchilla and Miles. Large crates of munitions were delivered there to be broken down into more readily usable quantities, repacked, and sent off to the conflict zones. The army bolts must have held the large crates together. This of course was at a time when Australia's government was seriously considering abandoning Queensland north of Brisbane if the Japanese invaded.

One benefit of the Yankee soldiers being there occurred on Saturday nights, when the GIs would be given leave to go into Chinchilla to the pubs or possibly dances. In those days there were gates where the road crossed the railway line and of course it was a nuisance having to stop and open them. Enterprising kids from the district would man the gates and open them for the soldiers on the way to town, usually being rewarded with a 1p or 3p. Of course, the return journey might be much more lucrative when the drivers were full of grog. Two bob (20 cents) was a king's ransom for a twelve-year-old in those days!

For my final two years of school, I boarded at Churchie, the Church of England Grammar School in East Brisbane. My two brothers, Jack and Lester, had bathed themselves in sporting glory there in previous years and so I was expected to continue the tradition. Sadly, it didn't happen. There was no polocrosse and my rugby union performance seemed to be blighted by the fact that I was as slow as a wet week and allergic to pain! I really did not enjoy boarding school—perhaps I was just a little bushie sook—but I did make several enduring friendships. There must also have been many interesting or amusing moments, but not a lot spring to mind, with one exception. Our science teacher, Jock, was a nice, old bloke, not really suited to teaching a bunch of smart-arse teenagers, but he did his best. The school had recently bought a moving coil galvanometer and Jock was absolutely thrilled with it. On several occasions he asked if we had seen it in action and although we had, we would always say 'no' to delay the actual lesson. Jock would then give us a demonstration. On probably the last occasion, one classmate asked, 'How much did that cost, sir?' Jock replied, with awestruck voice, '£300.' The classmate then asked, 'How much would a good one cost, sir?' Poor old Jock nearly wept as he replied, 'This is a good one!'

Like many people of my parents' generation, my mother and father had great respect for education. That does not seem unusual now, but life was different then. There were what were called the Great Public Schools (GPS) of which Churchie was one, and competition between them was fierce, both in the sporting and academic spheres. All of those GPS schools were private except Brisbane State High and I never realised until many years later that for a very long time State High was the only free secondary school in the whole of Brisbane, which in practical terms meant in the whole of Queensland. Of course, demand for secondary education at that time was not like it is today. Children could leave school and start working at fourteen, and many did.

There never seemed to be any push for my three older brothers to go to university, but by the time number four, Jack, came along, that seemed to be the way we were all expected to head. I did not really want to go to university; I wanted to be a racehorse trainer. You may ask why then did I not leave home and go to work for Tommy Smith or Bart Cummings to learn the trade and that is a fair question, but life was different then. Although I was born after the war, I was not a member of the 'baby boomer' generation, regarded by some as a generation of pushy, lucky over-achievers. They started getting born in May 1946, nine months after the war in the Pacific ended on 15th August 1945. Having been born on 22nd November 1945, I was a member of the 'Sit down, shut up and do what you're told' generation and so I went to university.

* * *

I can be a slow thinker sometimes and it is only quite recently that it has dawned on me what a serious disadvantage country kids suffered if they wanted tertiary education. The cost of living away from the family home was a serious impediment to many, if not most. I overcame this disadvantage by getting a State Government scholarship to study Veterinary Science. I really wanted to study law, but had not got a Senior (Year 12) level foreign language qualification, which was needed to get into the law course. I had done what was called an Industrial course for Junior. That included woodwork, metalwork and trade drawing but no foreign language. We were quite unaware that a 'language' was a compulsory requirement for most university courses, either at Junior or Senior level. Even the Veterinary Science course required a Junior language, so I studied Junior German in my sub-Senior year and passed, but Senior German in one year was considered to be a bridge too far.

UNIVERSITY

Anyhow, off to uni. Brother Lester and I and two other friends, cousin Bob and his mate Angus, shared a flat in Toowong for the first year and the two friends and I shared a different one in Taringa the following year. They both had diplomas from Gatton Agricultural College and had worked for a few years before coming to university. They had not done Senior but were permitted to enrol in Vet Science or Agricultural Science because of their Gatton diplomas. They were both pretty smart but, having never done Senior Physics, found first year Veterinary Science physics very trying. I recall one common Physics equation that contained the Greek letter omega, which these guys had never encountered in their lives, and they referred to it as 'little w'! Continuing the record of a lot of people who go back to university after spending some time in the workforce, they both graduated without ever having to repeat a year.

I passed through the Veterinary Science five-year course

relatively easily, albeit I had to survive a supplementary exam in Biochemistry in third year. Peoples' attitudes to exams always fascinated me. I would write all that I felt I usefully could to each exam question and when I had finished would get up and leave. My fellow students were a bit surprised by that and generally all stayed until the very last minute, hoping, I suppose, for divine inspiration. Perhaps they were right, because I mostly got passes and credits while many of them scored higher marks.

Australia was involved in the Vietnam War at this time and when I turned twenty at the end of second year uni, my birthdate was drawn in the conscription 'raffle'. I could have avoided the risk of call-up by joining the Army Reserve, which was called the Citizens Military Force (CMF) back then, for five years, but being eternally optimistic, and a bit of a dickhead, I elected to take my chance. At least my call-up was deferred while ever I kept passing my exams, and I really felt that the war would be over by the time I graduated. I couldn't really see what they were fighting about in the first place. You had to have shit for brains, I felt, to believe the 'domino theory', which predicted a sequential fall of all governments between Communist China and Australia unless vigorously resisted. Of course, the United States Military Industrial Complex, which needed wars to survive and prosper, and which President Eisenhower had warned about years earlier, was something I was totally unaware of. I was also unaware that the Australian Prime Minister, Menzies, believed in the domino theory.

There was always controversy surrounding conscription, the very reasonable argument being, if not enough people are keen to enlist, why are we going? Of course, it is fairly easy to make dispassionate decisions about such events when one is not the soldier getting blown up by a mine stolen from a badly sited Aussie minefield! The other point of contention arose about the issue of the lottery, rather than a call-up of all twenty-year-olds. It seemed unfair that some should have their lives totally disrupted while others would be unaffected, although, to be totally honest, I felt that I would rather have some chance of missing out than no chance. Anyhow, I chose not to think about it much before graduation. Didn't seem much point.

It has come to light recently that some very clever person (some might say smarmy prick!) who noted the favourable publicity that followed the drafting of Elvis Presley into the USA army, decided that it would be a good idea if Australia had a similar circumstance. This resulted in Normie Rowe, Australia's closest thing to an Elvis at the time, being deceitfully conscripted even though his birth date had not been drawn in the lottery. The son of the clever person revealed the deception in 2021 and, considering the outrage that innocuous events often seem capable of generating these days, I was surprised that there seems to have been not even a hint of a murmur.

Third year uni saw me move in with a new bunch of flatmates, or housemates actually, as five of us rented an old house beside the railway line in Toowong, dangerously close to the Regatta Hotel. There were four vet students and one bloke doing engineering at the tech. It was the technical college in beside the Botanical Gardens and was subsequently renamed, deservedly, The Queensland University of Technology. Anyhow, the tech student had acquired the nickname of 'Hot Tong' at school and was generally referred to as Hottie. Another of the residents was perhaps the most memorable person I have ever met. Warwick Smith was nicknamed 'Dapper' in perhaps the most egregious example of misnaming in world history. Top bloke, good sportsman, passed his exams, attractive to lots of women, but in your wildest dreams you would never call him dapper. An event that remains fixed in my mind is the night in the Regatta Hotel when Dapper, feeling the need to display his high regard of one of the barmaids, reached inside his shirt, pulled out a handful of chest hair, and sprinkled it over the woman as she leaned over to work the till. It's hard to imagine a more heartfelt endorsement!

There seemed to be a number of music bands with

unusual names around at that time. Perhaps there always are. Anyhow Dapper decided that if we were to form a band, an unlikely possibility as my guitar playing was our total musical qualification, it should be called 'Hot Tong and the Lesions'! Naturally, it never got off the ground but it does have one lasting relic. Dapper's beautiful girlfriend, later wife, was a regular visitor at that time and our sideboard still contains a 21st birthday present beer mug inscribed, 'To Scott from Hot Tong and the Lesions plus One'.

My brother, Jack, was working in Papua New Guinea at that time, but he was moving to British Columbia in Canada. He shipped some household items, including a washing machine, back to Australia to be stored until he returned. The gear was sitting in Swire's bond store and we expected to have to pay to have it released. My father sent down $20, which was about twice my weekly income at the time, hoping that would be enough. Dapper and I drove to Swire's in my old Holden ute one Wednesday afternoon—Wednesday afternoons were free for sport in those days—to pick up the crate. What a stroke of luck! We were not charged anything! That left $20 to spend as our reward. We managed to spend a fair bit of it on beer and arrived home well after dark. Dapper went straight to bed, but was soon feeling the discomfort, not uncommon in those circumstances, that attached to excess grog consumption. Naked as the day he was born, he went out onto our front landing for a hearty chunder over the rail. This then needed to be followed by the mandatory mouth rinse and drink of water so he went down to the front corner of the house to drink from the garden tap. One of the other blokes had his girlfriend visiting and when she was due to leave, they heard Dapper at the front, so elected to exit out the back and walk down the driveway. Dapper was leaning over the tap drinking when he saw the couple coming down the drive towards him. He might have been pissed, but he did retain some semblance of modesty, so decided to make a bolt for the front door. Unfortunately, some components of his physique were functioning better than others and he forgot to let go of the tap when he retreated, tearing it off the pipe it was supposed to be attached to. The next day we awoke to a veritable quagmire on the front lawn as the pipe had been gushing all night. The problem was sort of solved by hammering a bit of broom handle into the end. The big flow stopped, but there was a slow leak for months, bogging the odd unknowing visitor who chose to park on the front lawn.

One of the other vet student housemates also had a girlfriend who visited frequently, but the rest of us suspected that their relationship, at that stage at least, was non-carnal. Despite this, we were determined to embarrass him with the help of a new invention called a 'heat mount detector'.

This consisted of a small glass vial filled with red ink and attached to a small sheet of felt. Many dairy farmers had no bulls, relying on artificial insemination. The object of this device was for a dairy farmer to place it on the back of a dairy cow so that when she was 'on heat' another cow would mount her, which cows often did, and break the vial. This would signal to the farmer that the cow was at the right stage of her reproductive cycle to be artificially inseminated. As far as I know the idea sank without trace, but we had a bit of fun with it. The first stage was to accuse our housemate of having sexual relations with his girl, which he vehemently denied. The next stage was to pressure him into allowing us to put a heat mount detector under his mattress. In his innocent confidence, he readily agreed. The third stage was to say, 'Well, we have already put one in there, so let's go and have a look.' Of course, the device was already broken when it was placed, so we knew what the result would be. Vigorous denial and raucous hilarity greeted the unveiling. The romance did not suffer any kind of setback as a result of the ruse and the couple got married a year or two later.

The following year, fourth year, I moved in with a different bunch of vet students to a house only a short distance from the previous one, on Sylvan Road. You did not even have to turn a corner to walk home from the Regatta! We ate very well there. There was an arrangement by which selected members of three households would take turns to drive out to the Cannon Hill Meatworks and buy several sheep (dead ones, killed and dressed) to be consumed the following week. It was very cheap and the upshot was that our house had roast lamb four nights a week, two legs and two shoulders. This was also the time when I met my wife. I had been to a vet barbecue; each year group had one at the Moggil Vet Farm at the beginning of each academic year, and I had encountered an attractive, 6 ft tall, young woman, whom I took out to a subsequent barbecue. It turned out I was not going to get anywhere because she was the long-lost love of a student mate of mine who, not long after, became engaged to her. The engagement party was scheduled to be held at our Sylvan Road house. Not having a girlfriend at the time, I asked the six-foot engagee if she knew any mad-rooting females who might be lured to the party. Displaying an unbelievable lack of character assessment ability, she said, 'There is this girl called Flora where I work. She might be one!' Well, she bombed out there, but it didn't really matter because I was stricken at first sight. We met in February and married on the 25th of August that same year. Would you believe that, as I write this, it is almost fifty-four years ago! I know that there are plenty of people who have been very happy without having been married and produced a family, but I really think that they are only happy because they cannot conceive the joy they are missing. I do not pretend that it has all been blue skies and kisses, but it is a rare marriage, that is.

One of the most unusual things that happened to me while I was going to uni actually happened during the Christmas holidays at the end of my first year. I got a job as a roustabout with a shearing contractor for a job near Wandoan, about 160km away from my home at Chinchilla. My task was to sweep the loose bits of wool off the 'board'—the area where the shearers worked—and to be generally useful to the wool classer. On Friday of the first week, the shearers declared the wool 'wet'. It wasn't, but declaring it wet meant that shearing ceased and the men could all leave early for the two- or three-hour drive home. One of the other men, the wool presser, whose job was to put the various grades of wool into very large bales, got a lift home with me. Half-way home we stopped at a pub in Miles for several beers where Ronnie gave me an unusual lesson in reproductive biology. He explained that he had met his future wife at a bush dance in Boonarga (a very small village close to Chinchilla famous for having the world's only memorial, a hall, to an insect, the Cactoblastus, which eradicated prickly pear from Australia). He was not what I would have called a particularly attractive man, but I am not a female. After a minimum of urging, his future wife had accompanied him outside to the back seat of his car where two momentous events ensued. She was deflowered and she and Ronnie experienced simultaneous orgasms! On that basis Ronnie expected the girl to get pregnant. Who am I to argue? He drove her home to Dalby in the early hours of the next day and lo and behold, storming down the path to meet him was his old droving mate, Fred (or some name, I forget really). Fred said, 'G'day, Ronnie. This is a bit of a surprise,' to which Ronnie replied, 'Well, bugger me, Fred, fancy seeing you. I think I have potted your daughter.' Fred said, 'Oh well, Ronnie, time will tell.'

And it did. Ronnie said to me, 'I was right. She was five months pregnant when we got married.' How could I convince him it was a fluke? With the bountiful knowledge I had acquired in first year uni, I drew uterine horns, ovaries, spermatozoa and ova with a finger dipped in beer, all over the counter of the Queensland Hotel but to no avail. There was no way I was going to convince him. Practical knowledge beats academic theory every time!

NASHO

Flora and I married in August of my fourth year and it became increasingly obvious the following year that the Vietnam War was not going to end anytime soon. I graduated in December 1968 and was conscripted in January 1969. Recruit training for national servicemen, Nashos, was carried out at the Singleton, NSW, army base. The kindest thing I can say about it is that it was not a lot of fun. I also made a stupid mistake when the members of our intake considered possible officer material were gathered together shortly after training commenced, to be judged by a few regular officers on their potential. During the lunch break, one old Colonel asked me how I was enjoying the army so far. I replied, 'Seven hundred and twenty days to go, sir.' I suspect that that was not a good career move!

A further possibly fatal mistake I made was in shooting straight on the rifle range. Let me explain. At some stage later, I saw my confidential report, or whatever it was called, and saw that in our intelligence test I had got the highest score possible. On that basis, when we were given the opportunity to indicate our preference for the corps we would like to be sent to, I chose Intelligence Corps first, though not with any serious expectation of success. My second selection was Medical Corps, which as a veterinary graduate I expected would be a certainty. Sorry about that! Infantry! Mainly because most recruits could not shoot straight. If you are going to send a bunch of soldiers out into the jungle to kill Viet Cong, there is not much point sending ones who are going to miss. Of course, most of the conscripts were townies and had only fired rifles rarely, if at all, before coming to Singleton. One bloke, obviously smarter than me, explained his approach. He was a regular sporting shooter, but wanted to join the Catering Corps as he wanted to get into the food preparation business after his two years were up. He deliberately missed every time we went to the range, most of the time aiming at the stick which held the target up. Of course, he got his first-choice corps, because not many people willingly chose to become 'tucker fuckers'!

I don't recall if we ever got any local leave while doing recruit training, but we did often get it on weekends during corps training, which also took place at Singleton. We would usually go into the Singleton or Maitland RSLs to drink beer and play the poker machines. I did not have a vehicle there, but my good mate, Bob Fihelly, had an old Holden panel van and I often got a lift with him. I recall coming back to Base one night with him singing a song he knew about a parachutist, to the tune of John Brown's Body:

"They scraped him off the tarmac like a blob of raspberry jam,
They scraped him off the tarmac like a blob of raspberry jam,
They scraped him off the tarmac like a blob of raspberry jam'
And he ain't gonna jump no more."

It is ironic because, many years later, Bob got a helicopter pilot's licence and spent time helicopter mustering cattle in North Queensland before going to Papua New Guinea. There he worked ferrying Geologists around seeking various minerals until his chopper crashed. A piece of the engine broke off and flew up into one of the rotor blades and Bob was killed after the aircraft dropped 600ft. I'm not sure there would have been anything there to scrape off.

The Infantry Corps training took about three months. The final part involved a week-long exercise playing goodies and baddies on the top of Bulga Plateau, a geographical feature down Putty Road on the way to Windsor, an old town just west of Sydney. We arrived there in the late morning and spent several hours climbing to the top. It was quite steep and quite hard work. On arrival at the top, our object was to establish camp for the night, including setting up our 'hootchies'. These were small, two-man tents, made by joining the small, nylon sheets we had each been issued with, which were designed to clip together. The day was sunny and, even though it was late June, quite mild, so we made fairly desultory attempts to secure the hootchies, leaving them, in fact, quite susceptible to bad weather. Well, we got what we deserved! During 'stand to', the time at dusk when everyone goes to the perimeter to be on the watch for enemy incursion, the first drops of rain started to fall. And it never stopped and just got worse. By midnight, my hootchie mate and I were sitting up, back-to-back, huddled under the remnants of our 'tent', smoking to keep warm and shivering like dogs shitting razor blades. Our embarrassment at having unprofessionalism so exposed was only lessened by our discovery next morning that everyone else was in the same boat. The week-long exercise was supposed to be 'tactical', which meant that we behaved as if we were in a genuine war situation; however, the war was called off for a few hours while we built a great big fire and dried all of our blankets, etcetera.

Shortly after that exercise, we were all sent to our various postings. Many went to Battalions, but most of my mates and I were sent to Ingleburn, in Sydney, to the reinforcement unit. This was where we would stay until being sent to South Vietnam to replace other infantrymen who had either been killed or injured, got sick, or for some other reason got sent back to Australia. We basically hung around at Ingleburn until September, when we were all sent on pre-embarkation leave, after which the next move was to Vietnam. Unless you were a whinger like me. The day before we were due to fly out, I rang the Minister of Defence in Canberra and basically said, 'Fuck this for a joke.' On that basis, my movement was halted while some sort of investigation was carried out. After the dust settled, I was told, 'Sorry, old mate, you still have to go.' You can only be a conscientious objector if you object to all wars. You can't just object to one. I was finally shipped out in March of 1970. Perhaps I might have delayed the move by ringing Canberra again, but I didn't. The problem was that although I was opposed to the war in Vietnam, opposed to conscription, and definitely opposed to my being involved, I was in an environment where everything was geared towards getting soldiers to the war. I had to finally ask myself, 'Are you against going because you are against the war, or are you against going because you are just a cowardly prick?' Well, there was only one way to find out. I have read on a number of occasions since then that only volunteers went to the Vietnam War. Well, you can take it from me that it is complete bullshit!

I did have one enjoyable experience while I was based at Ingleburn and that was playing in the Queensland Polocrosse Championships. All soldiers scheduled to do overseas service are required to spend three weeks at the Canungra Jungle Training Camp just north of the Queensland-NSW border and in August most of my bunch went there. Because we worked the whole time, with only the middle Wednesday off, we were entitled to have two days leave to compensate for the Sundays we worked. There was no time off for working Saturdays. The Queensland Polocrosse Championships were scheduled to take place in Cunnamulla and one mate, who came from there, invited another mate and me to go. The Chinchilla polocrosse players and their wives had been like a second family to me and when they heard I was coming they left a spot for me to play in the second team. We drove overnight from Sydney to Cunnamulla after getting off on Friday afternoon, and I played two matches on each of Saturday and Sunday. And, we won the C Grade. What a ripper! Although I was probably the fittest I had ever been, I had not ridden a horse for a few years and the weekend exertions left me almost crippled with stiffness for several days.

There was also a second incident which bears relating: the story of the loose chin strap. We all wore slouch hats with chin straps which were meant to go onto the point of the chin, keeping them taut and the wearer looking shaped up. One of my fellow Nashos was seen by a passing Warrant Officer with his chin strap hanging loosely under his jaw. He was immediately admonished by the WO, but instead of instantly correcting himself, he took off his hat, threw it on the ground, jumped on it and shouted, 'Fuck this fucking hat, and fuck this fucking army!' Well, not surprisingly, he was put on a charge of 'insubordination', which is military jargon for having to front up to the senior officer of the establishment and be punished, if that is considered necessary, which in this case it sure was. I scored the job of being the armed escort. We lined up outside the Commanding Major's office building, me at the rear of the miscreant. With the WO giving the orders, we quick-marched two steps then two more up a low set of stairs, left-turned and marched three more paces before right-turning and marching a final three into the office where we left-turned, marked time and were finally given the order to halt. The charge was read out and the WO repeated verbatim what had been said. It was all I could do to stop myself from shrieking with mirth. The penalty was 30 days confined to barracks (CB). Had I burst out laughing, I might have scored a similar fate, 30 days CB for 'Refusing to take this bullshit seriously'.

For much of the time I was based at Ingleburn, Flora had a job. She used to catch the train at Liverpool and head into the city to work. I would drive in and wait to pick her up from the station when I knocked off in the afternoon. Usually there was time to have a couple of beers and I would buy one of the Sydney afternoon papers, of which there were two in those days. The *Mirror* was my favourite because, among other things, it contained a wonderful letters section where people could write to 'Dear Susie' for advice on all manner of emotionally challenging issues. The one that sticks most clearly in my mind was from a soldier based in Vietnam. He wrote to say that he had been overseas for six months and his wife had just told him that she was four months pregnant. His query was, 'Can you get pregnant through the mail?' Susie's reply was, 'No. I think you are the victim of a malicious pregnancy: someone has had it in for you!'

While I delayed my departure, I got some useful advice. It was suggested that because I was a veterinarian, I might get posted into Civil Affairs once I got to Vietnam, so it would be a good idea to get an army driver's licence. I thought that it might be an even better idea to have an army driver's licence if I didn't get posted into Civil Affairs, and that was how it turned out.

VIETNAM

I finally left Australia, flying Qantas, on 17th March 1970. For some reason we were not allowed to fly in army uniform, changing when we stopped briefly in Singapore before the final leg to Tan Son Nhut Airport in Saigon. The heat that greeted us in Saigon was extraordinary. There was very little humidity as the wet season was a couple of months away, but the heat was a real shock. Tan Son Nhut was at that time the busiest airport in the world, I was told, and I was not surprised. I have never in the fifty years since seen so many aeroplanes in one place. After a considerable wait, we were loaded into a Hercules and flown to Nui Dat, Australia's base camp in Phuoc Tuy Province. Flying in the Herc was a new experience—we didn't have individual seats but sat in rows on the floor with a big seatbelt stretched across us from one side of the plane to the other. Nui Dat itself was nothing to get excited about, particularly because after several months of dry season, everything was covered in dust.

There were twenty or thirty of us reinforcements, Reos, in this group and we went to the Reinforcement Unit (1ARU) which was adjacent to the 8th Battalion lines. The plan was for us to spend a few weeks being acclimatised before posting to various battalions. Part of the process involved pickets, as the perimeter had to be guarded 24 hours a day. It was not much fun on picket duty as you did two hours on and four hours off which always meant getting up in the middle of the night. There were always two people and the hours were staggered so one might go 2am to 4am and the next would do 3am until 5am. On my very first stint, having walked through pitch dark to get to the bunker (Nui Dat was in a rubber plantation), I found that I was sharing it with an ex-VC. That was a bit of a shock. There was a program called 'Chieu Hoi' designed to encourage Viet Cong to switch sides. Notes were dropped in the jungle and, no doubt, other methods were also used. The Chieu Hois would then come to Nui Dat to be reprogrammed. They were housed in the 1ARU lines. I doubt that many were genuine, but they had no trouble adjusting to our food. There was always cordial and often flavoured milk in the mess and the ex-VCs drank gallons of it. There was quite a drama surrounding one Chieu Hoi while I was there. He had confided to the others—I think there were four or five at the time—that he was going to get posted into a Platoon as a scout and kill his Platoon Commander, then go back to the jungle. At least one of the others was genuine because he dobbed the baddie in. The officers overseeing the process got a tape recorder, hid it in the Chieu Hoi tent and recorded the 'traitor's' words. He was reported to the Army of the Republic of Vietnam (ARVN) command who came and took him away, never to be seen again.

As well as the pickets, there were also lectures and demonstrations, culminating in a three-day exercise patrolling the jungle to our west. We were warned that the water we each took—perhaps three water bottles, I forget really, but it wasn't very much—had to last the whole time we were out. Foolishly believing this, I almost died of thirst living on tiny sips until it became apparent that half of the Platoon was completely dry and could not possibly survive another day without resupply. We found a stream nearby and filled all of the water bottles, hopefully staving off tropical diseases with Chlorine tablets, the taste of which ensured you only drank when absolutely necessary.

The second night was a revelation. We had left Nui Dat with two radios, called 25 sets; I think because they weighed about 25lb! Almost immediately, the handset of one fell apart. On night two, contrary to meteorological expectations, it briefly hosed down rain, somehow managing to fill the other 25 set with water. While that was pulled apart in an attempt to dry it out, we suddenly came under artillery fire! From our own side! Our boss, a Nasho Second Lieutenant, wasn't a bad, poor bastard, but obviously map reading was not his strong point. I say this in the assumption that the artillery gunners knew where they were firing; it was we who were in the wrong spot. Of course, under normal conditions that would not have been a major drama. We could have just radioed in to stop before they killed us. No radio made it a bit difficult. Moving was not an option because we had no idea where the next barrage might land. Our minds were taken off that issue though when one of the sentries thought he saw some baddies approaching and opened fire. All hell broke loose. I still suspect he fired at a figment of his trembling imagination, but it certainly caught our attention for a while. I know that the incident was registered as an enemy contact, but I remain unconvinced.

A day or two later, my mate from recruit and corps training days, Bob Fihelly, came to see me. He was attached to 5 Battalion and had just returned from an exercise somewhere in the Phuoc Tuy jungle. In relating the experience, which had involved contact with the Viet Cong, he said the VC had 'bookoo' mortars. I assumed that these were some new and destructive weapons, more dangerous than ordinary mortars, but declined to enquire. Several months later, to fill in time after driving my boss to Vung Tau for a meeting, I was taken in to one of the many Vung Tau bars by a mate who had been posted there. As I settled in and started my first beer, I was approached by a nice-looking Vietnamese bar girl. Apparently, one of the euphemisms for sexual intercourse was 'boom boom' and when I was offered bookoo boom booms, the scales finally fell from my eyes. The bookoo mortar was not a new and devastating weapon; there were just lots of them! As an ex-French colony, Vietnam had adopted several French words into their vernacular, including 'beaucoup'.

Most of the infantry reinforcements, called, in typical Australian fashion 'Reos', would be posted into Battalions part-way through their year-long tours of duty, so when the Battalions went home, the Reos stayed to finish their twelve months. Some went to other Battalions but many of my mates ended up at the Base in Vung Tau acting as guards. As well as being the Rest and Convalescence (R&C) centre and home of the hospital, Vung Tau was a port, so supplies came through there and all needed to be protected. It was a pretty good lurk to be posted there as it was relatively safe and the joys of the town bars were readily available. There were two types of bars. One lot were approved and the rest were not, for various reasons, presumably to do with security or sexually transmitted diseases. Of course, the men on R&C went to the approved bars because, even though they were more expensive, the Diggers only had two days, so the cost of grog was not an issue and anyhow they did not know any better. It was different for the guards though. They were regular customers, so they frequented the off-limits bars and off-limits brothels. Therein lies a very funny tale. One good mate of mine from Corps training was a Queensland bushie called Owen and he was sent to Vungers after his Battalion went home. Owie had managed to locate an off-limits brothel where his wildest fantasies could be played out for a very small fee. The locality was lovingly referred to as Three Buck Alley. One of Owie's mates was experiencing a prolonged period of depression, brought on by a belief that he could not satisfy women, so Owie was determined to solve his problem. He felt that the first thing he should do would be to take the mate to Three Buck Alley. As you can imagine from the name, this place had fairly basic facilities. The 'rooms' consisted of a bed and a very tiny space enclosed by blankets acting as curtains. Owen and his girl went into one and the mate went into the neighbouring one. For some reason, Owen's girl left for a while, so he wondered how the mate was getting on and decided to check. He peeped through a small gap in the curtains and was delighted to see his patient gleefully having it away. There are two things you need to know here. One is that the Vietnamese used the expression 'number one' regularly to signal approval. In the villages I often heard, 'Uc Dai Lai (Vietnamese slang for Aussies) number one, VC number ten!' The other thing you need to know is that Owie had a very large penis. It had once been described by an imaginative observer as being like a baby's arm hanging out of a cot with an orange in its hand! Anyhow, as Owen gazed on his mate, he got, and I quote, 'A gigantis bar'. He used to say gigantis instead of gigantic, but you get the message. He unveiled his erection and cheekily poked it through a gap in the curtains. Of course, the mate could not see it as he was face down, but the girl could. She shrieked, 'Number one! Number one!' to the delight of her customer, who thought it was a comment on his performance. However, when she started laughing, old mate knew something was wrong. It didn't end well. I don't think he attempted suicide, but I believe it did take a long while and a lot of beer for him to recover.

This is probably as good a place as any to tell another tale about Owie, albeit it happened back in Oz. He was living with his parents who had a grazing property on the Warrego River and they used its water to irrigate their lawn. His older cousin had a neighbouring property, but it had no river frontage, so he used bore water to irrigate his lawn. In that area, bore water came out of the ground very hot.

One of the boys was having a 21st birthday, so a big party was staged at the cousins' place. On day two of the party, Owie's mother prevailed on him to stop drinking rum for a while and eat something. As a rule, he never ate when he was having a big booze-up as he reckoned it made him sick, but on this occasion, he ate most of a chicken to humour his mum. True to expectations, it made him sick. The house had a big verandah which had no rails as it was only 50 or 60cm above the ground. Owie, who by this stage was wearing only his jockette underpants, got down on all fours and was vomiting over the edge when the cousin got a bright idea. He had an old kerosene fridge on the verandah which was fired up at party times to chill beer. Beside it was a five-gallon drum of kero and a funnel and a little hand pump. The cousin poked the funnel into the underpants and between Owie's buttocks and pumped some kerosene in. When it reached the sphincter it started to burn, so Owie headed for the lawn sprinkler, forgetting that he was not at home. According to his cousin, 'He dragged his arse across the lawn like a dog with worms and when he sat on the sprinkler his arms shot out and he trembled!' Owie had forgotten the bore water was close to boiling! Fully appreciating the merit of the trick, he never held a grudge.

There was one final exercise in the acclimatisation process when we went down via Chinook helicopters to an island called Long Son to act as guards in a public relations exercise. Aussie engineers were building a pipeline from the island's well back to the only village, a distance of maybe 3 km. This would save the women long walks every time they needed water, thereby 'winning the hearts and minds' of the locals. The worry was that the dastardly Viet Cong would sabotage the pipeline, and the engineers as well if they could. Our job was to ensure that did not happen. Of the three sections in the Platoon, each day one would guard the engineers, one would patrol to find a suitable spot to set up an ambush that night, and the third would stay behind at the camp we had set up. On one occasion I was in the section patrolling and found myself crossing a small clearing. We travelled in single file. Halfway across the clearing I heard a chicken cackle. Wild birds do not make a noise like that. Domestic chickens do. That was a serious worry for it indicated to me the probable presence of humans; and there was only one type of human likely to be in this vicinity—Viet Cong. Turning towards the noise, I saw a bunker on the edge of the clearing, about 15 m away, and I knew I was going to die. In retrospect, it was a strange sensation, because I seemed to be past fear. The overwhelming emotion I experienced was one of sad loneliness, that I was thousands of miles from home and loved ones, in the middle of nowhere, dying for a worthless cause I could do nothing about. This all took no more than one or two seconds and, thankfully, nothing happened! The bunker was empty! It seems the cowardly prick I had wondered about had surfaced, if only briefly. God knows where the chook had come from. The experience left me feeling quite angry.

Later on we stopped for lunch on the side of a short ridge. We could see below us several Vietnamese working in an area of open ground, cultivating vegetables as far as I could tell. One of the other guys on our patrol said, 'Look at that lot. I bet they are all VC (Viet Cong). We should shoot the bastards.' After my experience of a couple of hours earlier, I am not sure that if someone had opened fire, I might not have joined in. The high-profile case of American Lieutenant Calley who was responsible for wiping out half a village of civilians is well remembered. I cannot possibly condone what he did, but I think I can understand.

We all survived the Long Son campaign and, shortly after, most of my companions were posted out to the various Battalions. I remained at the Reinforcement Unit as a driver. I was quite happy about that although it was not long before boredom set in. That was exacerbated by the onset of prickly heat. This is a condition that affects many people when they first go to the tropics. Fortunately, it usually only lasts for a couple of weeks, but while present it is like having a mass of small spicules of fibreglass embedded in your skin! It caused me to do one of the stupidest things I think I have ever done. One of the regular driving jobs was to visit the food store and pick up supplies. On my first visit, I entered a very large cold room to help load perishables into the Land Rover and was delighted at the soothing effect that the cold air had on my prickly heat. Thinking that if a little is good, a lot must be better, I took my shirt off and luxuriated in the wonderful result, until of course I went outside to the real world. My prickly heat was then about ten times worse than it had been before I started!

About this time, Qantas had a promotion whereby people under twenty-six could fly to England at a special price and have a free Asian stopover. Flora's mother shouted her a ticket so she could go and visit her sister who had married a Pommie, so she blithely advised me that she was coming to Saigon on her way. I replied that there was a war on and there was no chance that I would be able to see her. She completely ignored my advice and sent me details of when she would be arriving. As luck would have it, the Administration Officer of the ARU was a veterinarian who had graduated from the University of Queensland a year before me and I knew him. Even more luckily, he knew Flora from when she had worked at the uni Sports Union. I think that because of this contact, and because my request was so unusual, I was allowed to go to Saigon. Nobody was permitted to have leave in Saigon, so we had to maintain the pretence that I was on some kind of duty. I was required to report in to Army Headquarters each morning of my three-day stay, but just register and leave. While Flora was there, we stayed at the Khach san Caravelle, the hotel where many foreign journalists stayed. I had wanted to stay at the historic Continental Palace Hotel, but it was booked out. On the couple of nights when I was in Saigon but Flora had not yet arrived, I stayed in the 'Saigon Canberra', an establishment in Cholon which had been taken over by the Aussies. One old Digger I met there was a Transport Corps Corporal who spent most of his days doing bugger-all at the Army Headquarters and he suggested that when it was time to take Flora back to the airport, he could come and pick us up. That sounded pretty good to me and so that was what happened. We got to Tan Son Nhut and had a couple of beers while we waited for Flora's flight to be called. The flight was delayed, so we had several more. The Vietnamese beer was, and probably still is, called Ba Muoi Ba, or Thirty-Three. In recruit training in Singleton my Platoon Sergeant had said that Vietnamese beer had embalming fluid in it! I naturally said, 'Bullshit!' Regular soldiers are terrible liars. But would you believe it, it's true. On the label it lists formaldehyde as one of the ingredients, and you can taste it. If you treat it the same as ordinary beer, it is not very nice, but the Vietnamese aren't stupid. They would get a big glass and put a big chunk of ice in it, then pour the beer in. As it cooled and diluted, it made the beer taste not too bad. Of course, the airport bars are much too sophisticated for that type of behaviour so the Thirty-Three sits in the fridge along with the Budweiser and Pabst, etcetera. Anyhow, by the time Flora left, old mate and I were well primed. He suggested that, rather than follow the regular route back to Cholon, we might take a shortcut down beside the edge of the airport. I was told later that there was some new special kind of aircraft down that way and it was all very secret, and perhaps that was true. On this occasion, there was a well-armed Vietnamese soldier blocking our way. As we tried to convince him to let us through, he seemed most reluctant to oblige. You have probably never noticed, but many army vehicles have little attachments to their bumper bars. These are perhaps 15 centimetres square and contain signs indicating the Corps of the vehicle or rank of the passenger. On this occasion, the previous passenger had been an Aussie Brigadier General, and rather than remove his sign, the driver had just enclosed it in a canvas envelope. Our Vietnamese guard moved around to the front of the olive-drab Holden and lifted up the envelope. Well, I was in civvies and so he had no real idea of my rank, but after seeing the red square with a silver star in the middle he jumped back, saluted me and waved us through. That was a bit of a highlight, but the next day I returned to Nui Dat.

* * *

Flora's visit to the UK was interesting for a number of reasons. She spent a bit of time in London with her sister's parents-in-law who were quite impressive people. Father-in-law, Maurice Green, had been the editor of *The Telegraph*, a famous England newspaper. I understand he occasionally had a smoko with the Queen! And his wife, Janet, had worked in Bletchley Park during World War II! I don't think it was she who deciphered the 'Enigma' code, but her just having worked there impressed me. I got a letter from Flora while I was in Nui Dat and she told me the Greens had been invited to a dinner party and the hostess had been concerned that there were uneven numbers as one of the guests was not bringing a partner, so Flora was conscripted to be paired up with Enoch Powell for the night! I did not even know who Enoch Powell was, but I mentioned it to a Pommie Corporal who worked in our unit and he was most impressed. Powell was a remarkable bloke in many ways, including his having been made a Professor of Ancient Greek at Sydney University at the age of twenty-five, but is best remembered for his 'Rivers of Blood' speech wherein he predicted serious problems if the immigration of blacks from the British ex-colonies was unchecked. He was roundly vilified for his racism, but a subsequent Gallop Poll showed that 74 percent of people agreed with him. That, however, did not stop Edward Heath from sacking him from the Conservative Party Shadow Cabinet. His prediction has proved to be quite accurate, but I believe we could learn more from a speech he made to the 1967 Conservative Party conference. In view of Australia's current standoff with China, one can only hope that Powell was not prescient when he said, 'History is littered with wars that everybody knew would never happen.'

I met the Greens years later when they visited Australia and had in the meantime been even more impressed when I saw a Hammond Innes book that had been dedicated to Maurice and Janet who had fished in the Hebrides with him. The Pommies take their recreation very seriously and fishing, particularly for salmon, is a major pastime, followed, for those with enough money or friends, by shooting and riding. I was dumbfounded when the name of some past high-profile Englishman came up in conversation and Maurice said, 'He had a dreadful seat on a horse,' to which Janet replied, 'But he shot very well, Maurice.'

AATTV

Back in Vietnam, apart from a bout of Shigella Dysentery which made me so sick I did not even want to smoke, life remained safe but boring until the end of June when I had the opportunity to move out of Nui Dat. I joined the Australian Army Training Team Vietnam (AATTV) as driver for the Major who was in command of the team in Phuoc Tuy Province. This involved a shift to a very large Army of the Republic of Vietnam (ARVN) training unit called Van Kiep, on the edge of the provincial capital of Baria, about 10km from Nui Dat. It consisted of a central compound occupied by Yanks and Aussies, surrounded by about 5000 ARVN Trainees, which meant that for me, sentry duty was a thing of the past. Because of the considerable amount of single-vehicle travel involved in the new job, the risk was significantly greater than in Nui Dat, but well worth it. One of the reasons, apart from no sentry duty, was that I got paid a daily allowance. The compound in the middle of Van Kiep was occupied by about 100 Americans and 20 Aussies. The whole AATTV exercise was under the oversight of the Yanks, and we ate in an American Mess, which meant that I had to pay for my food at every meal. This worked out pretty well because if I ate three meals a day it cost me about $1.50, but the allowance was a little over $5. This does not sound like much, but when you consider that cigarettes were 15c for a packet of 20 and a can of beer cost that as well, $5 per day was a king's ransom. And, in fact, if I bought Winfield cigarettes by the carton, they only cost 12c a packet. You couldn't afford not to smoke! The only problem was that, because the allowance was meant to cover actual costs, I could not bank any of it. It had to be spent. I managed. There were two bars in the compound; one for the officers, both commissioned and non-commissioned, and the other was for other ranks. I drank in the 'other ranks' bar. I was actually a lowly Private but got a field promotion to Corporal as the AATTV would not have anyone so menial as a Private! It was actually not too bad if you had to be in South Vietnam in a war, because on some weekends we stopped work at midday on Saturday and did not start again until Monday. The Mail Sergeant used to go regularly to Vung Tau where he was in contact with an Aussie soldier who doubled as a starting price bookmaker. We could hear Sydney and Melbourne races broadcast via

Radio Australia, so on occasional Saturdays we could have a few bets, numerous beers and play the poker machines in the 'other ranks' bar. The profits from the pokies were given back every couple of months via a free barbecue. This included free beer, which sounds pretty good, but had a catch. Apparently, the American system was that the percentage of the American beer market occupied by a certain beer brand in the USA would be the same percentage of total beer purchased for the troops in Vietnam. This led to a few anomalies where a particular quite unusual beer favoured by one locality in America would end up in an outlet where it was not appreciated. Such was the rationale for our free beer. The only way to get rid of this stuff was to give it away. It was called Black Label and apparently was drunk and loved in the wilds of Tennessee, or somewhere, but was bloody awful. Someone told me that it had lumps in it. I never actually swallowed one on the only occasion that I tried the brew, but it certainly gave the impression that there could be lumps there. At 15c a can, bought beer seemed a reasonable alternative.

Many of the towns and villages in Phuoc Tuy Province would have an ARVN unit attached. This usually comprised a well-fortified compound housing a company-sized unit, of perhaps one hundred men. The theory was that these soldiers would spend their days and nights patrolling the surrounding countryside looking for the dreaded Viet Cong. Whilst that happened sometimes, particularly in the predominantly Catholic towns, in many cases that commitment was observed in the breech. Men had to do twenty years of army service and many did not want to be there in the first place. The respect for Ho Chi Minh was not confined to North Vietnam. He had got rid of the French and now they had been replaced by other foreigners who had installed a puppet government. The more time you spent running around in the jungle looking for a fight, the more chance you had of finding one and getting shot, so why bother, particularly if your dearest wish is that the foreigners would go home and the war would end. The lack of commitment was highlighted for me by a visit I drove my boss to one day shortly after I started work with the Training Team, when he was scheduled to meet a Village Chief and his offsiders at their headquarters. Several of the Vietnamese were wearing black armbands. It turned out that the son of one of the local dignitaries had been killed by a mine a night or two before. He was VC! It takes a while to get your head around that.

Anyhow, the lack of aggression by the ARVN units was the main reason the AATTV was here. The plan was to embed a Mobile Army Training Team (MATT) with as many of the village compound units as possible. Each team usually consisted of a couple of Warrant Officers and three others, either Sergeants or Corporals. In theory they were there to advise, but in practice their role was to push the ARVN soldiers into being more proactive. When I started, we had four MATT teams and by the time I came home I think we were on the way to having thirteen.

Of course, these units had to be managed and the team members doing that lived in Van Kiep. There was a Major in charge, a 2-IC Captain (Hartley, who later became a General), a Sergeant who delivered mail and supplies to the teams, a Nasho interpreter who drove the 2-IC and became (and remains) a good friend, and me. There were other Aussies as well and I was never really sure what many of them did. There were a couple of funny (if you could call it funny) experiences though. When I joined the AATTV, I had to go to Saigon and be issued a full kit of American gear including a uniform and a Colt .45 pistol. I stayed overnight at a Yank facility called Camp Alpha where I found myself in the bar late in the day. There in the crowd was a group of four or five Negros enjoying themselves (they were called Negros then. They have since mutated through Blacks and Black Americans to the current, as far as I know, politically correct terminology of African Americans which makes me wonder what to call Americans of Egyptian heritage) and making a bit of noise, but not anything a normal person would mind. Beside me at the bar was a GI from the Deep South and he was fuming. He could not bear to see these black men enjoying themselves. He turned to me and said, 'They've got to be seen, haven't they? Man, if they carried on like that back home, we'd burn 'em alive!' They say travel is educational, well he certainly educated me!

I was most impressed with the Colt .45 and carried it in the Land Rover for a while until it occurred to me that if I really needed to defend myself, a rifle would be more useful, so the pistol got put in my bag under the bed. It did get brought out occasionally though. The Training Team Sergeant who used to deliver the mail, etcetera to the MATT teams had managed to find a local girlfriend, and he occasionally asked me to drive him into Baria so he could spend the night with her. To get to my vehicle, I had to walk past the Officers Bar, and it would have looked a bit suspicious if I was carrying a rifle at 8 o'clock at night, so I used to just put the .45 in my pocket. This happened several times until one of the other Aussies asked if he could borrow it. He was what was called a FOO, Forward Observation Officer, an Artillery Soldier who would accompany an Infantry Patrol and be able to accurately call in artillery support in the event of meeting enemy soldiers. When the FOO returned from his patrol, he told me the .45 didn't work! Apparently, the top of the magazine was bent and rounds of ammunition could not be released. That was the end of my nighttime drives.

Everyone past a certain age has heard of R&R. Rest and Recuperation, or Rest and Recreation, was an integral part of overseas service. During a 12-month tour of duty, a soldier would be allowed home, or somewhere else, for five days. In the country, there was also, for the Aussies at least, R&C, Rest and Convalescence. This comprised a two-day break at Vung Tau at some time during a 12-month stint. Finally, there was R&I. This was for the Training Team men and intended to compensate them for the fact that they were on duty 24 hours per day, 7 days a week, all the time. I think it entitled them to one day per month in Vung Tau and I am ashamed to say I do not remember what the 'I' actually stood for, though most suggested 'intercourse'!

The story goes that there were two team members who went to Vungers for R&I at the same time. One had a girlfriend whom he was going to marry and take home to Australia at the end of his posting. He was paying her so she would not have to work in the bars. The other had a similar girl whom he was planning to take to Thailand on R&R with him. He was not going to marry her, but had already given her money and a refrigerator to keep her out of the bars. These blokes got increasingly excited as they approached the locality in Vung Tau where their girls lived, until the final destination where they discovered that they had been paying the same girl. Of course, she had never stopped working in the bars.

On the coast of Phuoc Tuy Province was a mountain range called Long Hai. Many Australian soldiers were killed there by Australian mines which the VC had removed from a minefield further east. There was a bitumen road quite close to the beach joining the villages at each end of the range, but it had not been used since the Tet Offensive of 1968. One of the MATT teams was attached to an ARVN unit in the process of reopening this road in the latter half of 1970. Our overall boss of the AATTV was Colonel Clark and he insisted that all of our Land Rovers have sand bags covering the floors. They were quite heavy and slowed the vehicles down, but it turned out to be a good idea. A couple of the team members working on the Long Hai coast road drove over an M16 mine. These are the ones that were called Jumping Jacks—they jump out of the ground before exploding. None of the men were injured, but the vehicle was a write-off. It taught me a lesson about bureaucracy. In the army, there is a form called an L&D. This is what you fill out if you have lost or damaged some equipment. Most people's experience would be that if they reported the loss of some relatively minor item, the rigmarole they had to go through would be quite daunting to the extent that they would rather do without the lost item than go through the process. It was quite different with the Land Rover. My boss filled out his L&D form and the immediate response was, 'How soon do you want it?' They didn't say, 'What colour?' but probably would have if there had been a choice.

This mine event occurred at about the same time as the USA decided to bestow on the AATTV an American citation called a Meritorious Unit Award. This was a pretty big deal. Most team members gathered in Vung Tau for two or three days to rehearse the parade we would put on and the Northern Command band was sent from Australia to provide the march music. On the actual day, the Supreme Commander of the US forces, General Crichton Abrams, attended to present the award. After the parade, we all went inside and sat down while the bosses stood on stage and made various speeches. At the end, both national anthems were played. I am not sure that we Diggers saluted, but the blokes on stage did and I watched General Abrams have a heart attack. It was amazing. There is no surprise that he made General because he must have had extraordinary courage and discipline. He stood saluting and as I watched he turned grey and his face looked terrible. He did not flinch until the music stopped, and shortly after sitting down he was taken off to hospital.

That was September 30th and I was counting down to

my return to Oz. My boss, Major Phillips, was not due to go home until the following March and suggested I might like to stay on until he finished. I suppose I might have been thankful for the implied compliment but, if so, it was a very fleeting sensation. My friend Graham, the interpreter, and I arrived back in Sydney on a Qantas flight at 10pm on Christmas Eve. There was no flag waving, no 'Thank you boys for a job well done,' no nothing! Just an old Staff Sergeant, who wanted to be somewhere else and told us to turn up at Enoggera on the first day after New Year.

We did that and that was the end of my army career.

VET PRACTICE

Having been supported by a Queensland Government scholarship while I was at university, I was then bonded to work for the Department of Primary Industries (DPI) for six years after graduation. The two years of National Service came off my bond, but I still owed the DPI four years. I had actually been posted to the Animal Research Institute at Yeerongpilly for the month or so between when I graduated and when I went into the army, but I hoped to go to a country town as a Government Veterinary Officer when Nasho finished. This did not happen and so I resigned and went to Victoria to work as an assistant in a dairy practice in the West Gippsland town of Drouin. To be honest, I think I was going to resign no matter what the DPI did. I didn't want a boring government job; I wanted to heal the lame and the halt, even though it meant having to pay back some of the scholarship money I had been given. I have been told that the courts took a very dim view of bonded scholarships and I would never have been forced to repay the money, but I felt a moral obligation. Silly me! What's morality count when money is at stake?

Anyhow off we went to Drouin. On the way, Flora's cat escaped when we overnighted with some uni friends at Wodonga, so on my first day off we drove a couple of hundred miles back in my new work car, an Austin Tasman, to retrieve the feline. Halfway back to Drouin, in an ominous foreshadowing of future reliability, the car broke down. The Tasman was not as bad as the Austin P76 which came sometime later, but it indicated the direction in which the brand was heading.

In February of the second year in Drouin, our beautiful daughter, Penelope, was born, adding a whole new dimension of loving enjoyment to our lives, but it became apparent to both Flora and me that we would not stay in Drouin. Vet practice was a bit different back then and to set up a new one the tendency was to try and find a place where there was no vet. Those days are well and truly gone now, but we scoured the Australian Veterinary Journal looking for practices for sale. One advertisement was not for the sale of an existing practice, but an offer to assist establishing one in Alice Springs. The local Chamber of Commerce was offering subsidised accommodation if someone would set up there. It looked interesting, so I responded to the advertisement and was sent quite a bit of information, including a copy of the local paper to let us get an idea of costs and the general feel of the place. I was a bit taken aback to read the headline on the front page: "Shire Chairman admits, 'I might have been in the bush too long!'" Apparently, one councillor had suggested that the risk of flash floods washing unaware tourists off the causeway over the Todd River was so great that lifebuoys should be mounted on all of the guideposts in the danger area. The Chairman had agreed with the suggestion, but was quickly pulled up by another councillor who, as well as making the 'been in the bush too long' statement, added that the lifebuoys would soon disappear, only to reappear hanging off the backs of all the Territory Ringers' utes. The Ringers, hired stockmen from the various cattle stations, had scant respect for authority at the best of times and the temptation offered by such a novelty would be totally irresistible. The Chairman, chastened, admitted that his critic was probably correct, thus prompting the newspaper headline.

We seriously considered going to the Alice, but finally passed after having a look at where it sat on a map. Alice Springs is basically 1000 miles from anywhere! With one young child and the prospect of more, we just did not want to be so remote, so we ended up buying a practice at Wauchope, on the Mid-North Coast of NSW and arrived there in time to start work at the beginning of January 1973. My mother had died the previous year, and my father died very soon after we got to Wauchope. Circumstances prevented me from attending either funeral, but I found I could honour their memories and regret their passing in my own solitude. I would like to think that my children and grandchildren, at least, might be a bit sad when I finally 'tear up my ticket', but hopefully not for very long.

Inflation is a marvellous thing. The vet practice, including the house and stock, cost $22,000. We had a $4000 deposit and I worked seven days a week so in three years it was paid off, except for a small residual home loan. As well as bearing a beautiful boy in June of 1973 and then looking after both children, Flora worked as the Vet Nurse/Receptionist. Actually, the boy wasn't all that beautiful when he was born. He was an ugly little bugger, but he soon changed and started winning hearts and he's still doing it!

Working in my own practice was enjoyable and challenging but a one-man show becomes very tiring. I hoped to get enough business to employ an assistant, but could not seem to generate enough income. Of course, the main reason was that I didn't charge enough for my services, but eventually my opposition vet came to the rescue. Bill Walmsley was a tough, old bloke and had never got on with the fellow I had bought the practice from. However, he was an ex-serviceman and a keen follower of horse racing, so we became good friends. He had actually got First Class Honours and a Gold Medal from the University of Sydney and was going to work as an assistant to Sydney's top racehorse vet, but he developed an allergy to horse dandruff. For that reason, he opted for a country practice and when he came to Wauchope in the early 1950s, he was the only vet between Newcastle and Grafton. That ensured that Bill had all the work he could handle and no opposition vet, so he earned a reputation for being a bit gruff with clients who annoyed him. One such event bears relating. Sometime in the 1950s or early 1960s it was decided that Australia should eradicate the cattle diseases Brucellosis and Tuberculosis. The eradication of Brucellosis involved vaccinating all female cattle before they were six months old. Wauchope used to be called the Timber Town before some reformist government shut down the native forest logging industry and there were several small mills dotted around the district. It was not uncommon for mill workers to have a small farm in the vicinity of the mill and Bill was often called to vaccinate the usually small number of heifers bred on these farms. Unfortunately, because the owners were not always experienced cattlemen, their facilities were frequently inadequate. When someone phoned Bill to ask him to come and vaccinate his heifers, Bill would always ask,

'Have you got a race?' that is, a set of rails forming a narrow aisle where the cattle could be confined. If the answer was 'No', Bill would say, 'Call me back when you have built one.' He had been caught too often in time-wasting circumstances. On one occasion, he arrived on a property to vaccinate five or six heifers and was aghast at the 'race' he saw. It seemed to consist of one set of 10cm x 5cm rails about 60cm from the ground and another set about 60cm above them. They were about a metre or more apart, far too wide, and so it was going to be impossible to immobilise the animals, even if they didn't escape through the gaps. The male of the establishment was at the mill working and his wife had been left in charge. Bill asked her, 'What's that? An elephant race?' She was a bit indignant and explained that her husband had spent all weekend constructing it. Bill enquired if he had got any specifications and she proudly replied that no, he had built it out of his head. Bill said, 'I bet he had plenty of fucking timber left over!'

Well, that was the end of that visit. The Government Vet from Kempsey had to come and do the job, presumably after the race had been modified.

Bill had made quite a bit of money over the years and owned two farms, so he was not desperate to do a lot of vet work. He kept his old, good clients and I ended up with new ones and some his old ones whom he had upset. At one stage he tried to get rid of his practice, but it was really only half a serious concern, so not really saleable. After about four years I was getting sick of working too hard and confided to Bill that I was thinking of selling out and leaving. Partly because he liked me and partly because he thought Flora was wonderful, he sold me his practice which then allowed me to employ an assistant. He was going to give it to me, but I insisted on paying. The actual price was a carton of Tooheys Flag Ale and a bottle of Sparkling Burgundy!

Bill had several children including Paul, who decided that he would not bother working for a living when he left school; he would just go on the dole. This allowed him to spend his days with his like-minded mates surfing the beaches at Port Macquarie. This worried Bill, because, among other considerations, he had heard that the boys were eating Pal dog food as it was cheaper than regular food. This meant that there was more money left over for drugs. There were some encouraging signs though. Bill had a grazing property at Long Flat, a small town west of Wauchope, and he spent a lot of time there driving his little Suzuki 4WD ute around the hills spraying weeds. On one occasion he came across a stand of marijuana plants, which he correctly assumed to be Paul's. He explained to me that Paul would have to carry water several hundred metres uphill to water the plants and so he did not spray them. His rationale was that it was better for his son to be up there working than down at the beach eating Pal dog food with his dole-bludging mates. Marijuana is very susceptible to Roundup (Glyphosate) and so Bill had kept well away from the plantation, but spray drift apparently did affect the row closest to where Bill was spraying. The plants did not die, but the leaves curled up and did not look too good. Of course, Paul and his cohorts were dead against 'chemicals'! They were happy to sniff, smoke, ingest and inject all kinds of drugs, but 'chemicals' were a serious no-no! Therefore, come harvest time, Paul took the sickly plants and buried them before selling the rest to his 'fence' in Tamworth. Shortly after, I ran across Bill at the RSL Club and he was in good spirits. He explained that he had high hopes that Paul might finally become a productive member of society. He had made so much money selling his crop that he came back and dug up the sprayed plants. 'I think he is a capitalist at heart,' Bill said.

Paul's agricultural venture continued and seemed to be quite successful, but a few years later he was found hanged by his belt. Bill suggested that it might have been a practical joke that went wrong, but considering the business Paul was in, that might have just been wishful thinking.

Bill had been in the army in World War II and went to uni straight after. Because of his experiences, he was a keen member of the Returned Services League (RSL) and worked to ensure the success of the local RSL Club. In the days before poker machines, it was not easy for the club to make much money, so Bill came up with the idea of a non-profit raffle. This was a great success and ensured that the club was full every Friday evening, even long after the arrival of the 'one-armed bandits'. I used to go down at about 5pm and if I spent a dollar or two on tickets, I was almost certain of winning a prize; fish for the early winners then frozen chooks. I often had to take two or three snappers out onto the back lawn and scale them in the dark after I got home.

During these Friday sessions I occasionally had a beer with one of the local car salesmen named Jim. He was a cheeky little fat bugger and quite good company. On one occasion he told me about his friend who had a sexually voracious young girlfriend whom he was able to satisfy enthusiastically because he had a supply of hormone tablets. Jim, of course, then asked if I would be able to get some for him. I said I would see what I could do, but there was no way I was going to get real hormones for him. In his physical state, excess activity might be fatal. I can't remember what I finally got, but they were tablets which were basically flour. I told Jim that they would taste floury because they were a hormonal plant extract and he believed me at the time. I came across him several weeks later and he asked if I had really given him a genuine hormone. I said, 'Why, aren't they working?' to which he replied, 'Yes, they are, but I am not sure if they are working because they are working or they are working because I think they are working.'

Ah, the power of positive thinking.

The novelty of healing the lame and the halt wore off quicker than I ever expected which was a bit of a shame, but there were a few highlights. One involved Mrs Mitchell's cat. I had been told that the internal diameter of a male cat's urethra was linked to the male hormones in its body, therefore a tomcat that had been castrated too young is susceptible to urethral obstructions. I have never seen this confirmed in a peer-reviewed publication, but it does not seem unreasonable. Anyhow Mrs Mitchell's cat had a blockage causing it serious discomfort. I had read an article about a novel operation to correct this problem and decided to give it a try. The result was a spectacular success, inspiring me to write a song about it! The first and last few lines owe their style to Banjo Patterson's 'Man from Snowy River', but the rest is mine:

There was trauma at the surgery 'cos the word had got about
That Mrs Mitchell's cat might pass away.
For the poor beast couldn't piddle,
he was blocked up in the middle
Of the urethra, with stuff like curds and whey.

We tried to solve that riddle, how to make the pussy piddle;
The solutions they were varied and were many.
Someone suggested rebore, but that might make him too sore,
And of reboring tools, I hadn't any.

Well, his balls, I couldn't see 'em, so I incised his perineum
And gazing at his arsehole I exclaimed,
'I'll take the sick urethra and I'll run it out beneath ya,
I think that you'll be functional but maimed.'

His urethra I inspected and with scissors blunt dissected
Where it stretched away towards the pelvic rim.
Pulled it out then cut his cock off,
sewed him up so I could knock off,
Left him looking quite asexual but trim.

Now up at Ellenborough where the Mitchells make their home,
It's a small town, it's only got one shop.
Scores of tourists exclaim 'Really!'
as they watch the puss piss freely
And the Mitchells tell the story of his op.

My second memorable surgical event involved a young colt which my assistant had castrated. There had been no negligence on his part, it was just bad luck, but a whole lot of bowel herniated through the inguinal canal, which is the passage through muscles which testicles follow as they descend from the abdominal cavity.

On arriving at the property, I saw the colt in agony on the ground, kicking at a great bundle of intestines and I knew he had to die. I don't know why I did not just euthanise the horse immediately, probably because I had a weeping female owner beside me, but resolved that I must give it a go and try to fix it. I gave a general anesthetic and tried to assess the damage. If I made a circle with my arms, that is about the size of the ball of intestines that had herniated, so it was pretty daunting. They were covered in dirt and there was no possible way I could get them back, even if I had wanted to. Which I didn't, because there were several holes kicked in them. So, I cut the whole lot off! Then the plan was to join the two cut ends together. This was not as easy as it might sound because one end was small intestine and the other end was large intestine. The only solution was to stitch the large end over then cut a small hole in the side and join the small intestine to it. I did that, cleaned the site up as well as I could, then pushed the gut back inside and sewed the inguinal canal over and waited for the patient to die. For interest's sake, I laid the removed intestine out on the ground and measured it. Even with kinks in it, it measured 17 ft! I say feet instead of metres because my boots were exactly one foot (30cm) long so it made measuring things easy for people like me who still thought in pre-decimal terms.

Would you believe the horse recovered? I guess you would, because if he had died as I had predicted, you would hardly expect me to write about him. Honesty compels me at this stage to confess that the success does not reflect in any way on my skill. It was a very messy job and that the patient did not die of shock immediately or peritonitis later remains a miracle. Anyhow he never missed a beat.

(Note from Flora: Scott was a very good surgeon. I did not witness the above op. But his description surprises me a bit because he was meticulously neat and tidy when operating. He was very careful about asepsis, and worked fast and effectively. Of course, the horse survived.)

I have just one more veterinary story and it is not important because of the science, but it commenced the chain of events which concluded in my leaving veterinary practice. I had a client/friend called Richard Oakes who owned a racehorse called Bold Lyric. It showed a fair bit of promise and Dick sent it to a trainer named Ron Martin, who was based up the range west of Wauchope at the New England Tableland town of Walcha. Ron was quite famous in that he had a race named after him while he was still alive. The Ron Martin Maiden was a valuable race run at the annual

Walcha Cup meeting. This reflected the respect afforded to Ron—he was an excellent trainer and a very good bloke. Anyhow, Ron was concerned about Bold Lyric's knees, so Dick got me to go and look at the horse. There was no lameness or soreness, but the joints were a bit 'puffy'. This indicated that problems would occur if exercise was continued. I must say here that one of the hardest jobs a vet ever has is to convince the owner of a promising horse to give it a decent spell. Ron captured my attention by stating that, handled correctly, Bold Lyric might be a chance in a race like the Epsom. There are two big 1600m races run in Sydney each year, the Doncaster at Easter and the Epsom in the Spring. They are very prestigious and very valuable. Ron handled all of the young horses owned by the Nivisons, a wealthy Tableland grazing family, and would determine which should go to a Sydney stable and which should stay in the bush. His record was excellent and he really did know what a good horse was, so between us we convinced Dick to give Bold Lyric a good spell. Three months later he went off to a top Sydney trainer, Neville Begg.

After one conditioning run at Warwick Farm, Bold Lyric went to Newcastle and delighted us all by winning at 20 to 1! His next run was at Canterbury in Sydney on a Wednesday. I decided to 'big-note' myself and fly down. I had an assistant by then, so could leave for the day. Bold Lyric won again! How long has this been going on? A couple of weeks later he was due to race again at the Randwick mid-weeks. Flora decided that she was coming as well this time so we flew down the day before. Strolling through the shops on Tuesday afternoon took us past a jeweller in a large, new high-rise building. There was a ring in the window that caught our attention and we decided to have one made like it from a ring Flora had inherited. I expected to be visiting Sydney periodically as I had sent a horse down to be trained in Sydney as well, so I could call in to check on the progress. I shall come back to this story.

Bold Lyric won again! Whee Haa! Of course, he couldn't keep winning forever and he never did win an Epsom, but he was a very good horse and did win more races. My betting success continued for a year or more leading to some very good wins. I shall relate a couple because they might help explain why I gave up veterinary practice at the age of thirty-two. The Bold Lyric run of success resulted in my winning several thousand dollars which was significant money at that time; however, I resolved to proceed with caution and not take more than $200 to the track on race days. On the first Saturday of 1978, I went to Port Macquarie and lost my $200 fairly quickly! However, I had a strong fancy for a horse called Leonotis, so I booked up a $200 bet with a bookmaker I knew. Leonotis won at 7 to 2, so I collected $700. I then got a tip for a filly in Melbourne called Tincture. She was racing first-up from a spell, but had good form in the previous Spring, so I had $100 each way at 16 to 1 the win and 4 to 1 the place. She duly won so I collected $2200. I had drunk several beers by now and was filled with confidence leading into the last race in Melbourne, where I had a very strong fancy for a mare called Belle Marie. I had $100 each way at 10 to 1 with five bookies and $50 each way with one who refused to take the $100. She bolted in and I won over $8000 for the day! I was paying my assistant $10,000 for the year at that time. Two weeks later I went back to Port Macquarie and was very keen on a horse called Jacaranda Lad racing at the Sydney mid-weeks. He had shown great promise as a young horse, but his form had tailed off a bit. I suspected that the probable cause was some unsoundness and so expected him to run well on the predicted wet track where there would not be too much pressure on his legs. I thought he would be about 3 to 1 and so was pleasantly surprised when he opened up at 5 to 1. I backed him and then the odds lengthened. Anyone with any brains would usually take that as a sign that something was amiss, but not yours truly. I backed him all the way out to 12 to 1, collected about $5000 when he prevailed, and used the money to buy Flora a Datsun 120Y station wagon. Funny thing is, I had a veterinary drug representative who used to call in every few months and who was a mad keen racing fan. He visited not long after and when I bragged about my success, he explained that a friend of his was a part owner of Jacaranda Lad and he had not even gone to the races that day because he knew the horse did not handle wet tracks! Just luck on my part, but I was convinced that it was skill.

This led to my seriously considering my future. If I was that smart, why would I persist in a job where I had to work long and unsociable hours for not a lot of reward when a lucrative alternative was staring me in the face. Actually, I wasn't completely stupid. But I was getting very sick of vet practice. I tightened inside every time the phone rang; I had not drunk red wine for a year or so because of its effect on my gut; I had more recently stopped drinking white wine for the same reason and was eating a packet of Quik Eze per day.

There were a few amusing interludes though. The horse I had sent to Sydney injured a leg and had to be spelled, so my expected regular visits did not eventuate. In the meantime, there was no word from the Sydney jewellers about our ring and I did not even know their name. I knew where they were and had expected that I would just walk in there to check on the progress. After a few months had elapsed I started to worry, but help was at hand. Our local solicitor, Bill Glass, was a good friend who went to Sydney every now and then and he was a great fan of the Danish silversmith, Georg Jensen, who had a shop just opposite our jeweller. Bill often visited there so I asked him if he might call in at the jeweller opposite and find out how our ring was getting on. I expected just a casual inquiry, but Bill arrived and said something to the effect of, 'I am Bill Glass of solicitors J M Glass and Son and am here to inquire about my client's ring!' Well! That caused a bit of a stir. The ring arrived in the mail about a week later, a very satisfactory job, and we are still waiting for the bill! I kept promising myself that I would call in next time I was in Sydney, but my horse broke down and I never got there before we left NSW.

* * *

Being involved in the racing industry meant meeting a list of memorable characters, including the President of the Wauchope Race Club, Colin Maxwell. We were discussing horse doping one day and he told me about a good old horse he used to race which won him enough money to buy his first refrigerator. He was considerably older than I was and he was referring to a time before stewards swabbed winners to check for illegal stimulants. You could buy caffeine from the chemist; it came in a twist paper like a lolly wrapper. Colin said, 'He was a good old horse, but you had to shout for him.' He used to start him in a race early in the program—horses often raced twice in one day back then—but without the caffeine. The horse would do no good, so when he started in a later race, his odds would be quite long. This was when the caffeine was administered. Apparently, he loved it because Colin said that when he heard the wrapper crinkling, he would start to salivate and lick his lips! The conclusion was that, contrary to popular misconception, doping did not hurt the horses because this one lived to the ripe old age of twenty-six!

I had another indelible experience in racing after my trainer's apprentice jockey rode his first winner on my horse. I had seen this animal racing without success locally, but he always looked awful. I had the bright idea that I might buy him quite cheaply, improve his looks and performance and profit from the exercise. The first part went okay; worm treatment and supplements made him look pretty good. After a couple of encouraging conditioning runs, we took him to Wauchope where he won, to my great excitement. I'm glad I got some excitement that day, because it was the last time I got any from that horse. His name was Finish Fighting which I hoped signalled that he would finish each race fighting to win. Sadly, the opposite was the case. He was finished with fighting! It took a couple of runs for that to sink in though, and at his next start after he won, the same apprentice jockey rode him amid great expectations. This boy's father was also a trainer and actually had a horse in the same race. He did not want to win though because he wanted more success for his son, so he had given his jockey instructions not to pass my horse. By the time the field was leaving the back straight, it was apparent that Finish Fighting was not going well and the father's horse actually won the race. Afterwards, he said to me that he had given the order not to win, but his horse had drawn level with Finish Fighting and his son had told the other to go for his life because he was travelling so poorly. He then said to me, 'It's good when the boys can work together like that, isn't it?' I laughed and wondered if the Stewards would share that view.

The previously mentioned Richard Oakes had several friends who were members of the Port Macquarie Repertory Society who negotiated a deal with a newly-opened restaurant, the Clockwork Orange. For providing entertainment to diners, the Society would receive some payment, so I was asked to go and sing a few songs. We had a lot of fun, but it was never going to last because the food was awful! One night I attracted the attention of a woman significantly older than I was who seemed to think she was a serious contender. Bugger me! The upshot was that I wrote a song, sort of based on the experience. I cheated a bit because to have a 'groupie' you really need to be in a group, but I claim poetic licence.

My Groupie's on the Pension

When I first started singing there,
I thought things would be swinging there
And the groupies would all flock right in to greet me.
But what a let-down, matey, I only score one, over eighty,
It seems the rest would rather die than meet me.
Well, the first night that I played
she was the only one who stayed
And she hobbled round to meet me at the bar,
Wiped the dribble off her chin, then she really got me in
When she cackled, 'Boy, I think you'll be a star.'
Chorus:
My groupie's on the pension so she hardly rates a mention,
But I suppose that she beats none at all.
At 83 she still moves fast, thinks each one might be her last,
And she's so grateful I feel ten feet tall.
Next verse:
I don't think she'll last a year, but she's a horny bit of gear,
And I'm gonna stick with her through thick and thin.
The old folks' home's where she hung out
And now she's got me so wrung out,
That when her room-mate dies I'm moving in!
Final Chorus.

BACK IN QUEENSLAND

I sold the vet practice to my assistant and left for Queensland on the first day of Spring in 1978. Flora was seriously unhappy about the move, but did not fight it too much. Her mother had died a couple of years previously and her father had followed her recently, so our plan was to stay in their house in Warwick until we found somewhere to go and the house was sold. I had not intended to stay in Warwick, but we did. I bought a farm a couple of miles out of town and proceeded to waste a fair bit of time and capital racing horses. I guess honesty compels me to relate a racing story which reflects very badly on me. I was at the Gold Coast yearling sales as I used to cart yearlings there in my truck to help pay for it. On this occasion, a good mate asked me to put in a few 'dummy bids' on one of his horses. The idea is that he will not sell for less than, say, $8000, so I might push the bidding to just short of that figure. If someone then raises the bidding, the animal will be sold. If not, it will be passed in. Sounds fairly simple, and it is, unless you are half-pissed, almost asleep, and bid on the wrong horse! So, I ended up with an animal we named Early Bid. Funnily enough, she had quite a lot of ability, but soundness issues were a problem.

We kept the first farm for a couple of years and sold it for a good profit but then, being a slow learner, I bought another one. It gets worse. Having spent the previous eight years working with dairy cows, I had reached the conclusion that you had to have rocks in your head to be a dairy farmer, so what did I do? Bought a dairy farm!

It took three more years before reality finally bit. The children were growing up and we wanted to send them to private schools. That could not possibly happen with what I was earning milking cows, so in 1984 I got a Government Vet job with the Queensland Department of Primary Industries. I was based in Roma and commuted for three months before Flora and Sam came to Roma. Penny was at boarding school.

Working in the DPI was a bit of a revelation. I had always regarded public servants as a different breed from the rest of us and, to be honest, a bit inferior because of their easy work practices and emphasis on job security. How stupid was I? They were mostly pretty good blokes who worked hard and I became good friends with several of them. I used to enjoy the morning tea break, when everyone gathered in the smoko room to discuss, argue and banter about recent events. It quickly became apparent that Rugby Union was a serious issue. Roma fielded a team, the Echidnas, in the local competition and a few of the staff either played or were seriously committed followers. Every Monday morning smoko would see prolonged discussion about the previous weekend's performance. There were conversations about what the team had to do to get into the semi-finals and win so they would make the final and it all sounded very complicated. Until ... one day I discovered that there were only three teams in the whole competition. St George, Charleville and Roma! Despite that, there were some exciting moments. Watching Roma vs St George, I observed an obviously very keen ex-player, ex because of a broken leg still in plaster, hobbling along the side-line. As his team equalised the score at three-all after scoring a field goal, 15 minutes from full time, he was heard to shout, 'Okay, St George, now consolidate!' Shortly after, Roma scored a try and the cheers were so loud that our broken-legged friend's little dog joined in and started barking, which earned him a kick in the ribs for being unpatriotic.

Much of my work in Roma related to the Brucellosis testing of a large herd north of Wallumbilla. This was part of the national Brucellosis and Tuberculosis Eradication Campaign (BTEC) which had also involved the vaccination of all heifers less than six months old. Brucellosis was a disease that caused abortion in cows (hence the name Brucella abortus), but it was also a Zoonosis, meaning it could also affect humans; for example, if they drank unpasteurised milk from an infected cow. It was not common in humans, but most unpleasant for those unlucky enough to get it. There are other forms of the organism as well. British soldiers in Malta in the 19th century died from drinking milk from goats infected with *Brucella melitensis,* which fortunately did not make it to Australia, and pigs have their own Brucellosis as well, *Brucella suis.* This does not seem to cause much trouble in pigs, but can give confusing positive blood tests in cows that have been exposed.

Testing involved blood samples being taken from all cows on the Wallumbilla property and in this case, there were more than 2000 cows. Things were looking good as we completed our bleed on the last mob to be tested, a group of young cows. All the tests up to then had been negative, so we were filled with optimism. Misplaced as it turned out. One animal returned a positive test. It was the weakest reading that could be rated positive: genuine positive tests were generally very strong (estimated by successive dilutions of the sample which still give positive results). One explanation for such a result was that the animal had been vaccinated when she was too old. The reason heifers were vaccinated only up to six months of age was that if done older, they could give a positive Brucellosis test result, albeit only a weak one. In large herds it was inevitable that the odd animal would get the needle when it was over six months, but most people were very careful. In case you are wondering why bull calves were not vaccinated, the reason is that transmission of the bacteria occurs only via milk or aborted foetal membranes, neither of which males produce.

Vaccinated heifers were identified by a three-holed ear punch and we anticipated being able to see the earmark in our positive animal. Sorry about that! No holes, therefore no vaccination. Our last resort was to try and find evidence of *Brucella suis* on the property as that could explain the weak positive test. I shot a couple of wild pigs and sent blood away to the laboratory. It tested positive and *Brucella suis* was subsequently cultured from lymph nodes. Thank Heavens! The property could now be declared clean.

I do actually have another Brucellosis story that relates to my time in Wauchope private practice. Horses can get *Bovine Brucellosis*, but in a strange way. Where ligaments run over bone, nature often provides a fluid-filled sac, a bursa, to ease the friction from movement. In horses there is a major ligament running from the top of the lumbar vertebrae all the way along, right up to the head, helping to stop the horse's head from falling on the ground. Where this ligament passes over the vertebral spines of the withers (just in front of where a saddle sits) there is a bursa. This could sometimes get infected with *Brucella abortus*. When that happens, it acts like an abscess and breaks out periodically. This is referred to as *fistulous withers*. Draining the abscess never seems to cure it as it seals over until the pus increases enough for it to break out again. Blood supply to the bursa is very poor and so treatment with antibiotics is never successful. I had a grazier call in one day to ask if I knew of any cure. He had a good stock horse which used to have its fistula break out regularly every three months. Coincidentally, I had just read about an injectable animal worm treatment, Levamisole, which also showed signs of being an immune stimulant in low doses. I had no idea what the dose rate might be, so as an experiment I gave him a syringe filled with 10 ml of Levamisole, with instructions to inject 1 ml under the skin every second day ten times. The bloke came from west of Kempsey, so was not a regular client of mine and I did not see him again for over a year. He did call in one day though to tell me that his horse was cured. He had waited twelve months before he was confident there would not be a recurrence, but after that felt certain. I was delighted to hear the news, but my cure was never destined to make me famous. Brucellosis has been eradicated, so *fistulous withers* hardly ever occurs anymore. Bugger!

CHANNEL COUNTRY

Two years after going to Roma I was encouraged to apply for a better job in Charleville. The Divisional Veterinary Officer would oversee the Stock Inspectors and Government Vets in that region. So, for not a lot more money there was a considerable increase in responsibility. Anyhow, I got the job and off we went to Charleville. We moved into a government rental house which was identical to hundreds of others dotted around the state, except that the water system was different. Charleville's town water came from a bore and it reached the surface boiling hot. There was a 200-litre cooling drum under the house which the water flowed through before it made it up to the upstairs kitchen or bathroom. The other unusual feature was that there was no lawn. Instead, there was a healthy growth of Buffel grass about waist high. I determined to smarten the yard up, so I borrowed the back hoe from the Pastoral Laboratory where I went to work each day. For some reason, the handle bars of this machine were about 40cm from the ground, requiring me to bend right over to work the machine. I don't know if you have ever worked a back hoe, but they are a bit tricky. When you get to the end of a row, you can't just casually stop and turn around. As the hoe is hoeing, it is dragging itself along so at the end of a row, you have to quickly lift the handlebars up to get the rotating hoe out of the ground, then quickly spin around and drop it again. This is probably no big deal if the handles are at a sensible height, but my ridiculously low handles meant I put my back under severe strain each time I turned. Eventually I strained my Sacroiliac ligament. It was not too painful at the time, but I knew it would be sore when I cooled down. And I was right. Next morning, I could not get out of bed. The ambulance had to come and strap me onto one of those folding stretchers to carry me down the stairs and off to the doctor, who helped me explore a whole new dimension of agony by attempting to fix my problem by manipulating my pelvis. This was a spectacular failure, so he sent me off to hospital where they gave me a shot of Valium as a smooth muscle relaxant and a shot of Pethidine. The doctor's final question to me had been something like, 'Apart from the excruciating pain, are you comfortable?' to which I replied, 'Not too bad, but I guess I will have to go to the lavatory at some time.' This led him to conclude that I badly needed to go, so when I was laid out in my hospital bed, they put a steel bedpan under me! I did not protest violently because the drugs had stunned me a bit, but there was no way that I was ever going to use that bed pan! I decided after a while to have an experimental attempt to get out of bed. There was one of those metal triangles which hospital beds often have hanging down and so I grabbed it and tried to pull myself up and over to the edge. Most of the time if you do something and it causes pain, you stop and the pain ceases. Not with Sacroiliac strain. It hurts and so you stop trying to move, but the agonising spasm takes a minute or so to die down. On this occasion, I had been allotted a male nurse to keep an eye on me, apparently. He was a good, poor bugger, but one of those nice, decent, naïve types, a member of a local Christian Outreach clique of some kind. As I tried to pull myself up, he thought I was trying to defecate, but having a lot of trouble, so he was offering encouragement. As I slowly and tentatively dragged myself up and across the bed, he was shouting, 'Go for it, mate! You can do it!' I did not appreciate the humour of the situation at the time but have laughed a hundred times since when remembering.

The Charleville Division's area extended south past Cunnamulla to the NSW border, north to Longreach and Winton, and west to South Australia and the Northern Territory. It encompassed much of Queensland's mulga country and almost all of the Channel Country. The majority of our work revolved around completing the national project to eradicate Brucellosis and Tuberculosis from the cattle herd. The closer settled properties were almost all clean, but there was still quite a lot of activity on the stations further west in the Channel Country, mostly because of Tuberculosis (TB). These were properties with areas measured in hundreds and sometimes thousands of square miles, and finding every last possible infected animal was a serious challenge. The problem, from an epidemiological point of view, was that if one beast in a mob of 1000 has TB, the whole lot are regarded as infected. Testing was useful in most cases, but sometimes, because of difficult terrain or recalcitrant stock owners, whole herds had to be destocked. In quite a number of cases there would be unmusterable animals, so they would be shot, usually from helicopters. This was always a big, expensive exercise, but not without its benefits. The pilots would be urged to drive fat cattle into the open where the choppers could land safely and the shooters could salvage the prime cuts. This was theoretically illegal, but nobody really cared. We ate fillet, rib fillet and rump but the cheaper cuts were usually ignored. One useful piece of information I learned was that if you want to eat steak in the first 24 hours after the animal died, and before the meat has 'set', the diaphragm is least tough. It's not tender, but it's better than the better cuts.

The population of the Channel Country is quite small, but it had far more than the usual proportion of characters. One was Windorah cattleman, Sandy Kidd, a legend in his own lifetime. Sando claimed to be the first person to muster cattle with an aeroplane and nobody disputed this. A friend of his, Bill Kelly, who had worked in the area years before I met him, on Cape York Peninsula, told two amazing stories. The first was that he and Sando used to go into neighbouring stations with absentee owners, and give them a bit of a hand removing unbranded stock, mostly scrubber bulls. The absentee owners were never made aware of this assistance. Sando would fly over the area and indicate to Kelly where the cattle were. Kelly's job was to ride there and run each bull on his horse until it was tired enough for him to be able to jump off his horse, grab it by the tail and pull it over. He would then sit on it and tie the back legs together with a belt specially made for the job. It sounds a bit amazing, but it is what really happened in many places, not just illegal exercises. They would then go and get a trailer and load the animal, or animals if they had got more than one, into it and bring it back to Sando's yards. On one occasion, Kelly made a miscalculation. He jumped off his horse and grabbed the bull's tail before the bull was properly tired. He could not pull it over, but was not game to let go as there were lots of small 'whipstick' Mulga trees around, none big enough to hide behind though. Fortunately, Sando flew over and saw what was happening, so he landed and helped save the day! Only problem was that he could land through the whipstick Mulga but could not take off. They had to spend half a day cutting trees down to let Sando leave.

On another occasion, the duo was trapping cattle on a dam. The dam wall had broken, but there was still some water in the bottom and they could see that a small mob was drinking there regularly. They installed a trap yard in the gap in the wall and managed to catch twelve or thirteen cattle of various ages and sexes. Sando had an old Bedford truck on which he had fashioned a stock crate and this was going to be used to remove the stock. They all got loaded into the truck, but it seemed that it was not powerful enough to drive up the dam wall in forward gear. Therefore, Kelly drove the truck up the wall in reverse and Sando helped by pushing from the front with his Toyota ute. When the truck reached the top of the bank, Kelly signalled to Sando to stop pushing because he did not want to go straight over and down the other steep side. His plan had been to turn the steering wheel hard and reverse along the top of the bank. Two things conspired to defeat this plan and cause a bit of a disaster. One was that Sando's crate extended past the back axel further than crates usually did. The second was that Sando did not stop pushing in time. So, the truck went straight back over the bank causing the cattle to fall to the back. Their weight levered the front of the truck up around the back axel, and it also lifted up Sando's Toyota which was entangled by its bumper bar with the front of the Bedford. The two vehicles were stuck together up in the air like a couple of fighting praying mantises. Meanwhile, because the truck was tipped up so far, the cattle all jumped out over the back of the crate and fled, and finally, Sando and Kelly had to walk miles to get a tractor and pull the two vehicles apart.

One of the properties where we had some trouble with the TB eradication program was Mooraberrie, north of Betoota. The main reason stemmed from an historical event in the early 20th century. The Queensland Government had apparently guaranteed a supply of beef for the British soldiers in World War I. To ensure this happened, they banned the sale of cattle interstate, contrary to the rules of the Australian Constitution which guaranteed free trade between the states. The Duncans, who owned Mooraberrie, traditionally sold their cattle into South Australia. Apart from anything else, it was the closest market, but they were prevented from moving the cattle south.

There was considerable acrimony and bureaucratic interference and finally the Duncans sued the Queensland Government for damages. The head of Queensland's

Supreme Court ruled in their favour; on appeal, the full bench of that court ruled for the Government; and finally, the High Court ruled for the Duncans. At that time, the highest court for Australia was the Privy Council in England and so the Queensland Government appealed again to that body. Ultimately, they got what they wanted and the ruling was in their favour. Needless to say, the chance of ever getting a Duncan to cooperate with a government disease eradication program was absolutely zero. By the time I was there, Miss Duncan, the spinster owner of Mooraberrie, had moved to a nursing home and the manager was a good, old fashioned, ungainly-looking bloke called Arthur Churches. I guess he had worked his way up into the position. The reason is disease related. There is a weed that grows in that region, *Birdsville indigo,* and it causes a condition in horses called Birdsville disease. The animals lose control of their back legs and ultimately die. For that reason, in the early days when horses did most of the work, the turnover was quite high. Arthur brought replacement stock horses up from South Australia on a number of occasions and eventually stayed. People do not get rid of their best horses so, no doubt, many of the ones Arthur bought and brought up were buckjumpers, or worse. Therefore, he had to be able to ride well. It was said that he looked like a bag of shit sitting on a horse, but he was very hard to buck off.

Arthur was inclined to continue the Duncan reluctance to cooperate with the government, but relented when it was pointed out that Mooraberrie disease status meant that his neighbours were disadvantaged as well. His basic decency was to my advantage.

Arthur was one of the 'old school' and there were few luxuries both at the homestead or in the camp. I was told that when the men were working away from the station and camping out for any length of time, Arthur would take an onion with him. Each day when a stew was being prepared for the night's meal, he would take the onion out of his pocket, peel one layer off and drop it in the pot, wrap the onion back up in a tissue and replace it in his pocket, thereby earning the sobriquet of 'One Onion Arthur'!

He was a good old boy, but quite ignorant about much of the world outside Mooraberrie, including some of the big words. It is useful here to explain that fattening cattle on grain—lot feeding—only became common in Australia from about the 1970s. Prior to that, in times of drought, stock would be sold to areas where there was feed or sent to meatworks, even if they were in poor condition. If an animal is severely undernourished, it affects the *rigor mortis* process and the animal will be condemned for 'malnutrition'.

Arthur had trouble understanding our obsession with TB in the cattle because they only had the occasional animal condemned, 'put down the chute' for it, at meatworks. He explained to me that the only time they had a lot of bullocks condemned was in a big drought when twenty or so were 'put down the chute for lalmutrition'.

On another occasion when I had to visit Mooraberrie, it was during school holidays so I took the family with me. Arthur invited us up to the house for lunch. Of course, tea was provided with the meal. Many old bushies drank tea with no milk and often no sugar. Arthur was one of them, but he did find some sugar when I asked. Not many of the western stations had house cows for milk, but many did use powdered or condensed milk, so I asked Arthur if he had any. He replied, 'What are you making? Pudden?'

Speaking of house cows reminds me that Australian cowboys and American cowboys are completely different species. We all recognise the American cowboy, but the Aussie one is usually someone who worked around the homestead to do the vegetable gardening, milk the house cow, and do other menial odd jobs. Not a romantic role and really not many stations have one these days. However, one Channel Country Station I spent a bit of time on did. It was Nappa Merrie, which belonged to the Stanbroke Pastoral Company, a subsidiary of the very big AMP insurance company. The cowboy was an alcoholic who went by the nickname of Sparrow. He had been a good sportsman in his youth, but had seen better days by the time I met him. On one occasion, the 'big boss' of AMP, Sir James Balderstone, whom they all referred to as JSB, was due to fly into Nappa Merrie for a brief visit, but the manager was urgently required at one of the outstations. Sparrow was entrusted with the responsibility of meeting and greeting JSB and was given a description so he could be easily recognised amongst the other passengers. The plane landed and passengers got out. Sparrow made a beeline for JSB who was apparently quite impressed at being recognised so quickly. He asked Sparrow, 'How did you know it was me?' and Sparrow replied, 'They told me to look out for a little, borley, fat cunt.' Well, there you go! Couldn't miss him, could you? It is appropriate here to explain the word 'borley', which is often used in Queensland to mean bald. Hereford cattle have red bodies and white heads, which make them appear bald (sort of). That is why they are often called borleys. I have never heard them being called baldies. Just thought I should explain that.

Another Sparrow story relates to the time when the relatively new lessees of the Noccundra pub got him to be their 'locum' publican while they took a holiday. They had met him a few times when he had called in briefly, but had no idea that he was a hopeless alcoholic. At a later date they told me that they didn't mind so much that he gave free beer to all his customers, it was the cartons of stubbies he gave away as they were leaving that almost sent them broke. I guess there are alcoholics and alcoholics, but Sparrow's explanation to me that the best thing he ever drank was methylated spirits with carbide in it—but you had to drink quickly before the bubbles stopped rising—put him in a class of his own!

Sadly, not all of the Channel Country stories are funny. About 80km west of Windorah, a couple of hundred metres on the northern side of the road, are the remains of JC's Hotel. It is just a pile of rubble now, but there are some gravestones which survive. One of them marks the grave of a young woman, 17- or 18-years-old, who died there. The inscription is particularly poignant. It reads:

"Shed not for her the bitter tear
that fills the heart with vain regret.
Tis but the casket that lies here,
the soul that filled it sparkles yet."

What a beautiful sentiment. It makes me think that she must have been a lovely person to inspire such writing. I made some enquiries and it seems she had come from Tasmania originally and she had committed suicide. Why would a beautiful, young woman commit suicide in that kind of environment? The obvious answer is that she was pregnant. The attitude to illegitimacy has changed a lot in the last 50 years, but the social stigma it attracted was severe and cruel for a long time before that. I have a counter-intuitive theory that the change was due to the advent of the contraceptive pill, even though that should have decreased illegitimacy and therefore increased its stigma. When I was a kid, in the 1950s, lots of people went to church. Churches of all denominations were violently opposed to 'fornication', particularly in the form of pre-marital sex, which suited the average mother and father very well. They didn't want their unmarried daughters getting pregnant. Lots of parents were embarrassed to talk about sex, which led to the publication of 'helpful' booklets explaining to youths how masturbation made boys weak and sickly and, in the case of the one that mysteriously appeared in my bedroom, girls with small breasts were frigid. The word 'orgasm' never rated a mention. You couldn't make this up! Apart from ridiculous publications like that, sex education was virtually non-existent, so the alternative was the threat of eternal damnation offered by the church.

Of course, it was not the fornication that was the trouble, it was the bastard babies. With the advent of oral contraception though, attitudes to sex completely changed. Whilst it wasn't actively encouraged, overcoming the threat of illegitimacy allowed people to acknowledge that sexual intercourse did occasionally occur and, surprise, surprise, it could actually be fun. Following on from this was a recognition that mistakes happened and it was not the baby's fault if its parents were not married. Illegitimate children and their mothers came to be accepted as normal members of society, but too late for the girl at JC's Hotel.

On the subject of illegitimate children, I am reminded of one of our Charleville neighbours. When introducing himself, the man of the household said, 'People call me the Phantom.' That was a bit strange I thought, but it paled into insignificance next to his daughter. She was a very skinny young woman; not a bad bird and a good worker, I was told. She had been working at a local service station and one of the customers noticed that she was showing obvious signs of being pregnant. When asked who the father was, she replied, 'I'm not too sure. I got a bit carried away the night after Railways (a local rugby league team) won the premiership!'

The Channel Country is famous for the quality beef that is produced there. Carrying capacity is low, but the areas are vast. Much of the pasture is not produced by rain, but by floodwater coming down from the better rainfall areas to the north. Before the Europeans settled there, water was only available in rivers and creeks, which meant that pasture more than a day's walk, or hop, from water never got eaten. As dams and bores were created, access to this feed meant the numbers of animals a station could support were much greater than would otherwise be the case. Kangaroo numbers also increased. In the decades leading up to the end of the 19th century, there was a succession of good years and stock numbers kept increasing. By the time of the Federation Drought, which encompassed several years either side of 1900, properties were bursting at the seams. I have been reliably told that Bulloo Downs went into the drought with 50,000 head of cattle and neighbouring Nockatunga Station had 35,000. At the end of the drought, Bulloo Downs had none and Nockatunga had 1000 bullocks! In those days, by the time drought was well and truly established, the stock routes were eaten out and cattle could not be moved. There were none of those dreadful carbon-dioxide-spewing road trains back then; just planet cooling, death by starvation!

The Channel Country is an area serviced by three rivers: the Diamantina, the Cooper and the Bulloo, which is the most easterly. The Bulloo does not go to Lake Eyre like the other two do in good seasons; it usually ends up in Bulloo Lake, in a big paddock on Bulloo Downs Station, just north of the New South Wales border. In a really high rainfall year, it can overflow into part of northern NSW; the area is called The Overflow and it was the home of Clancy, the subject of a couple of Banjo Patterson's poems.

Another well-known Channel Country property was 'Ourdel', a station right next to Windorah run by Sandy Kidd. Sando was quite famous for his aerial mustering skill, but he also rescued the Queen Mother one time when she was cut off by floods. I do not know if it was just those two things alone, or other positive achievements as well, but at one stage he was invited to Government House and awarded an MBE! Rumour has it that at the garden party following the presentation ceremony, Sando ducked off into the bushes for a piddle and lost the medal!

Never mind. Sando was smart enough to buy a big mob of sheep just before a mini wool boom at the end of the 1980s. He used New Zealand shearers. Some years before, there had been a big protest by the Australian Shearers Union about the Kiwis using wide combs on their shears. There had been complaints claiming the shears would cause injuries, but I think it was just about protecting jobs really. The other advantage offered by the Kiwis was that they were prepared to work different hours from the Aussie shearers. Instead of the traditional 9 to 5, the Kiwis would start at maybe 7am and finish by 3pm, which was an advantage in the hot summer. Anyhow, a team of Kiwis turned up at Windorah and startled the locals because there were several women included. None shore, but they worked as roustabouts in the shed. I need to tell you here about an old wives' tale prevalent in my childhood. It seems to have fallen by the wayside now, but there was a belief that sleeping or working in a draught, ie. a breeze coming through a crack caused by a door left partly open, would give you a 'chill', possibly leading to a more serious respiratory condition. The second year of Sando's sheep venture saw me passing through Windorah and I ran across Matey Richards, who had been working as Sando's Wool Presser. It must have been a weekend because he was not working that day, but I asked him, amongst other things, if the female roustabouts were back that year. He replied that they certainly were; in fact, there were even more that time. To quote him, 'There's that much crack on the board you could catch pneumonia from the draught.'

Another risqué tale from the west relates to a woman of a 'certain age' who had always lived in that area and was well known for introducing young ringers to the joys of sexual intercourse. On one memorable occasion, during the celebrations following the Windorah races, she and her latest inductee were seriously engaged in amongst the Spinifex on a nearby sandhill when they became temporarily disconnected and the young bloke's pride and joy hit the dirt! Undeterred, he attempted to climb back in the saddle, but was admonished by the memorable statement, 'Eh, boy, that's a cunt, not a cement mixer!' That was told to me as a true story, but I cannot vouch for it.

I did actually have another unusual experience in the Channel Country. When the Brucellosis and Tuberculosis Eradication Campaign was first introduced, there was a lot of discontent because of the extra work involved and the movement restrictions imposed on infected or suspect properties and the DPI staff were frequently criticised. As a public relations gesture, one of the Stock Inspectors arranged for DPI stockies and vets to run the bar at the Betoota races. This was quite successful and I was determined to participate when the time came. In the first year, I noted that the Queensland Government had donated enough money for a large, galvanised iron shed to be built, with the Stewards' and Jockeys' rooms at one end and bookmakers at the other. The original toilets were a short distance away, and to avoid confusion were signed 'Urinal' and 'Arsenal'!

Things were much different the following year. A massive wind had swept through and destroyed the shed completely. The steel uprights had been concreted well into the ground, but it looked as if God had come along and lifted the whole thing about 30 m into the air and then just dropped it. There was not a single piece of metal that was not bent. Because of some dispute over insurance the shed could not be moved which boded ill for the annual race day; however, the locals are not easily deterred. They built another racecourse a couple of kilometres away! A bunch of us, DPI staff, turned up to run the bar and the Secretary approached me and told me that they did not have enough judges. She asked if I could help and, of course, I agreed. You may not be aware, but judging is a bit tricky. It is no trouble when you bet on a horse because you follow it easily, but without a photo finish camera it is impossible to pick all placegetters accurately. Therefore, there has to be one judge for each place. It is also important to be elevated as otherwise the numbers get obscured. We three judges all stood on an old bookmaker's stand, which was slightly better than useless, but not much. It was about 40cm off the ground when we needed 4 or 5m! The first race was run and there was a tight finish with three or four horses crossing the line with less than a length between them. It was a debacle! Fortunately, the race commentator knew what he was doing and when our incorrect numbers were put up, he told the crowd that there was some mistake and the correct numbers of 3, 6 and 2 would appear shortly. Thank heavens we took his advice! You would no doubt expect the judges to be impartial and I guess they usually are, but Betoota is a long way from the mainstream. Most of us would have had a bet in most races, but you would expect us not to advertise the fact. However, in the main race one of my fellow judges startled me when he started cheering for his horse halfway down the straight! Fortunately, I think that with all the noise I might have been the only one who heard him.

I do recall another couple of Channel Country stories that are worth telling. One concerns a bloke who was a sort of roving Electrician based in Birdsville. I say roving because with a population of about 100, Birdsville township could hardly expect to provide an income for a tradesman of any kind. He drove one of those tiny Suzuki utes and the sign on the door said it all. "Someone or other electrical, we might be rough but at least we are expensive!"

The other tale relates to a couple of blokes from Quilpie who did contract mustering. The early settlers were Duracks and Tullys and while there are no Duracks still in the area as far as I know, there are still Tullys. One Tully man went into partnership with a chap called Watts and formed Tuwatty Enterprises, Contract Musterers. It is useful here to explain the word 'twat'. In England that word is pronounced to rhyme with 'cat' and signifies a stupid person. In Australia it is a slang word, one of many, for female genitalia, and pronounced to rhyme with 'hot'. Consequently, the local joke was that Tuwatty Enterprises was so called because wherever they went, they made cunts of themselves!

Our TB eradication work often involved the use of helicopters, sometimes to check that paddocks had been mustered well and no stragglers were left behind and sometimes to shoot unmusterable stock. On one memorable occasion, when our work was over, the chopper pilot stayed back in Windorah to do some mustering for one of the big company stations. He was able to stay in a caravan that the local Stock Inspector used, because he had gone on leave. On the Saturday after the station job was finished, the pilot and the station manager got together in the Windorah pub for a serious drinking session. Unfortunately, there was a new policeman in town. The local copper (it was only a one-copper town) was on leave as well, so a locum had been brought in from a distant but larger place. This new bloke was worried that the station manager was drinking too much and should not drive. He may have been better off keeping his concerns to himself. Anyhow, one thing led to another and the locum ended up getting a bit of a belting. Eventually, the manager drove home and the pilot went to bed in the caravan, but sometime in the night, police reinforcements arrived. Sandy Kidd told me later that the pilot must have been very drunk and fallen off his bar stool many times because he turned up on Sunday covered in bruises!

The police contingent drove out to the station to have a chat to the offending Manager, who pleaded guilty to the previous day's offence. He was given an on-the-spot fine of $100 which he did not dispute and the money was passed on to the locum copper as compensation for his pain and insult. Justice was seen to be done and justice was done. No lawyers, no magistrates and no appeals to higher courts. Should be more of it!

I was in the Charleville area for two years and it was interesting, but two years were about enough. I had been whinging and bitching and the powers that ran the show decided the best solution was a move. Cairns was the destination and that sounded pretty good to me.

CAIRNS

Flora and the kids left Charleville for Cairns in January 1988 in time for them to start in their new school. Both had been at boarding schools in Brisbane, but there was an excellent school available in Cairns which, amongst other things, was going to save us a considerable amount in fees. The children enjoyed their time there and made some enduring friendships with, as it turned out, some remarkable kids. I left several weeks later and took a three-day train trip to get there. Three days are enough on a train!

My work mostly revolved around the TB eradication program on Cape York Peninsula. Contrary to almost nightly assertions by the ABC weather lady, it was Cape York Peninsula, not Cape York, which is the tiny little protuberance at the top of the peninsula. Okay, got that off my chest!

By the time I arrived, the prospect of eradicating TB on many of the properties via a testing regime had been pretty well abandoned. The Aboriginal places, particularly, were not progressing. The country was very difficult and, to be honest, the Aborigines were not all that enthusiastic. They were lovely people and allowed you to put words in their mouths about their enthusiasm for the campaign, but when the chips were down, their hearts were just not in it. The bottom line was that if we wanted to eradicate TB, we had to eradicate the cattle. So that was what we did: mustered and sent off the marketable cattle to meatworks, and shot the rest. At one stage, as we were racing to meet a self-imposed deadline for achieving a particular disease status, there were twelve helicopters operating on Cape York Peninsula, all carrying Stock Inspectors and the odd Vet, shooting unmusterable cattle. Sounds a bit horrendous, but it worked. Australia is now free of *Bovine tuberculosis* and the inbred Shorthorn cattle that occupied the Peninsula for 100 years have now been replaced by Bos indicus animals which are tick resistant and much better suited for the tropics.

The Channel Country had its fair share of characters, but if anything, the Peninsula had more. I mentioned Bill Kelly earlier when he was in the Channel Country, but by the time I met him he was actually working on the Aboriginal property, Aurukun. He had been engaged in the early days when it had been expected that a testing program for TB might succeed. Kelly was the Livestock Manager. He told a lovely tale about when he had first arrived. On the side of the canteen, where all the beer was stored and sold during opening hours in the late afternoon, there was a gauze-enclosed 'bird cage' area. History never related what its original function was, but it was easily broken into, and once broken into, provided easy access to the inside of the canteen and all the stored beer. Break-ins were a fairly regular event. As part of his plan to develop a viable cattle program on Aurukun, Bill had brought with him a couple of electric fences. He set one of them up in the bird cage in such a way, he maintained, that someone could break in, but they would be trapped by the live wire and not be able to escape. He was very pleased with himself and expected all kinds of kudos from the local management. Sorry about that! On the very first night that his trap was set, it caught a burglar. Apparently, he was entangled in the live wire and spent some time yelling and cooeeing before being released. Kelly was summoned to meet with the Aurukun Council under the big mango tree at a specified time the next day. Expecting to have praise lavished on himself, Kelly was dismayed when the Shire Chairman severely criticised him, saying, 'Our people are not animals. You cannot use that cattle thing here.' Kelly replied that he thought they would be pleased that he had caught someone breaking into the canteen. However, his

Aurukun education began in earnest when the Chairman said, 'Our people have been breaking into that canteen, Kelly, long before you ever came to Aurukun!'

The original plan had been to use the electric fences to make a series of paddocks, which would allow cattle to be tested and segregated and eventually a clean herd might be produced. Unfortunately, it was never going to happen. If locals were going fishing and came across a fence where there wasn't one before, they were quite likely to just cut the wire, drive through, and leave the wire down. That made it impossible to segregate animals of differing disease statuses. After several years of trying, we gave up and decided to destock. As in the Channel Country, this involved mustering what could be mustered and sending them off to abattoirs, and shooting the rest.

On one occasion there was a team of stock inspectors based on Aurukun and my Brisbane boss, John Walthall, on a visit to the north, was keen to meet with them and see what progress was being made. Bill Kelly had a unit, half of a duplex, in Aurukun and the stockies were camping in the other one as it was empty at the time. John and I camped with Kelly, who decided to have a barbecue in honour of his visitors. It was a Friday night and the local Murris were noisily enjoying an extended Happy Hour in the bush not far away. Later in the evening, one of the stockies pointed to a young Aboriginal girl who had been standing in the shadow of a big Stringybark and throwing small twigs at the stockies to attract their attention. As far as I know, none were tempted, but a funny thing happened the next morning. Kelly had a regular offsider named Herbie Hooker, who was a 'yella fella', ie. part Aboriginal and part Chinese ('fella' is pronounced to rhyme with colour). Anyhow, at about 8am, Herbie turned up and kind of skulked around the unit for a while, until Kelly asked, 'What do you want, Herbie?' Herbie replied, 'Can I borrow a six pack of Fosters? Doesn't have to be cold. Hot ones will do.' Of course, there was then an inquisition. 'What do you want a six pack for?'

Well, it turned out that Herbie had come to an arrangement with the young lady who had been trying to attract the attention of the Stock Inspectors the night before. A tryst was scheduled, but he could not take her to his place because he was living there with another woman. So, the plan was that the girl's boyfriend, who had a motor bike, would take them both to some distant bower where congress would occur. The beer would be divided—two cans for Herbie, two for the girl and two for the boyfriend. It might be hard to believe, but it was all true. We laughed, but it was not really a laughing matter. It was tragic, really.

The manager of Aurukun was a white bloke called Bill Wightman. Funny that. Anyhow, we looked like getting stuck in Aurukun for a day or so, so he volunteered to take us fishing down the Archer River. It is very wide where it runs past Aurukun and we motored until we reached a likely spot, stopped and caught a couple of Barramundi, then headed back to town. On the way, I could see what looked like an abandoned tinny or something on the far bank. But it wasn't a tinny; it was an army duck. Many years previously, the good Samaritans of Melbourne had heard that the natives of Aurukun could not get around in the wet season, so they decided to help out. They found an old amphibious jeep—an army duck—got it going properly, and drove it up to Coen so it could be formally handed over to some representatives of the Aurukun community. Politicians and media attended to make the most of the event and it was all very wonderful. The dreadful wet season isolation (which the locals had been happily coping with for probably thousands of years) was now a thing of the past! Anyhow, when the festivities had ceased, the two or three local recipients jumped in the duck and headed for home. When they got to the Archer River they just drove in and motored across. How good was that? Unfortunately, when they got to the other side, they tried to drive out up a very steep bank and the vehicle overturned. The men got out and walked back to Aurukun, and the amphibious jeep has been lying there ever since!

One of the peninsula properties that I sometimes visited was Bromley, north of the Wenlock River, owned by a bloke called Ted Youngman. Bromley was interesting for a number of reasons. Many years before I was in that region, an American had contracted to buy the property for $300,000. He paid a $50,000 deposit which, instead of being kept in trust by the solicitor, was released to Ted. At the time, it was estimated that the place carried 1600 head of Tuberculosis-free cattle. The actual number was not mentioned in the contract, but the TB-free cattle on the property at settlement were included in the contract. The American on-sold 75 percent of the place to another buyer and that contract stipulated 1200 TB-free cattle. Ultimately, both parts were bought by a Victorian who sought delivery. In the meantime, someone had decided that Bromley might be a perfect place from which to launch satellites and much talk ensued about a space base there. According to Ted, BHP approached him and offered $1,000,000 and said they would take care of the existing contracts! Of course, Ted agreed, but unfortunately the Greens and the local Aborigines protested so much that the idea of a space base was abandoned. So, he went back to finalising the previous contract. There was a slight hitch. Since the original was signed, Bromley's TB-free disease status had been lost. A test and slaughter program did not seem like a viable option, so we destocked the place. This meant that when settlement occurred, there were not 1200 head of TB-free cattle included, there were none. This quite alarmed the Victorian buyer, not surprisingly! He went to the DPI headquarters in Brisbane trying to find out how his cattle had been moved. I received an inquiry from head office about the issue and, having seen the original contract which had only said the cattle present at settlement and not given a number, I faxed a reply to that effect, saying, '... and if the buyer thinks he is going to get 1200 head of TB- free cattle out of Ted, he must have two penises, because he couldn't get that silly playing with one.' Well, the buyer knew more about the law than I did. It appears that when the deposit was released to Ted, that constituted 'settlement' and the subsequent expected payment was more of a financing arrangement. Ted was taken to court and was bankrupted by having to pay for 1200 non-existent cattle.

Several years later, I came across another DPI vet who had recently been to a workshop teaching the intricacies of Freedom of Information legislation. The class had been provided with several examples of the type of thing that should be avoided. My fax was included! Many years earlier, Flora's sister, Rosslyn, had told her eldest son about me, 'He cannot ever be a good example, he can only be a terrible warning!' I hate to admit it, but perhaps she was right. The Victorian had submitted a Freedom of Information request and had seen my fax!

Bromley had previously been free of TB, but there were essentially no fences separating it from a neighbouring infected property so its ultimate downgrade status was pretty well inevitable. When that had happened, I had to visit and examine a strange, separate block. Sometime in the distant past, a separate lease had been created within Bromley, for a fairly large area. It was completely enclosed by Bromley, had no fences or infrastructure and nobody really knew who owned it. Ted just treated it as part of his lease. For bureaucratic reasons, I had to determine its disease status which just involved driving through the area and confirming that it was, for all practical purposes, really part of Bromley. My visit coincided with school holidays, so I took my son, Sam, with me. We picked Ted up from his house and drove to the area in question while Ted regaled us with tales of his life, including the 'letter in a bottle'. Several years previously he had been mustering cattle beside the beach and as he rode near the water, he saw a bottle which he stopped and picked up. It contained a message from an American dentist who dropped it from a cruise ship on which he has been getting a free trip in exchange for being the ship's dentist. Ted left school at a very early age and could not read, but his wife could, and so then Ted dictated a reply which she wrote and sent off. Shortly afterwards, the dentist sent his reply which included, amongst other things, an invitation to visit him in California, where he said that if there was anything he could do for Ted, he would be delighted to oblige. I could not help but laugh at the dentist's offer because Ted had probably three original teeth in his whole mouth. No false teeth at all, just the three!

There is a weed that grows on Cape York Peninsula called Marpoon bush, *Morinda reticulata*. It is interesting because it accumulates Selenium and if eaten by horses causes their hooves to drop off. I had often seen it growing beside the road and it did not look very palatable, so I asked Ted about it as we drove along to examine the strange block of land. He explained that it was one of the first things that grew after rain and the horses would eat it then. He said that it was a nuisance as they would duck back and forth to get a mouthful as he rode along and, to put it in Ted's words, 'It's as if they get dictated to it.' Sam almost burst as he tried to stop himself from laughing.

Cairns is a beautiful place and we had a good time there, although it does get a bit humid in summer. Thirty-two degrees is balmy in Charleville, but combined with 99 per cent humidity it can be really oppressive in Cairns. You do get used to it though and after a while we settled in and got ourselves involved in the community. Flora joined an orchestra and I joined the chorus of a couple of Gilbert and Sullivan shows. It was also while we were there that I resigned from the National Party and joined the Liberals. I had been a fairly enthusiastic follower of politics from the conservative side for years, but the goings-on of the Joh Bjelke-Petersen regime, which had run Queensland for decades, were exposed and I was quite dismayed. In retrospect I couldn't help but be a bit bemused, both by my reaction and the reaction—still in existence—of the media. When Joh was finally defeated, Queensland had no debt. Compared with the $80 billion profligacy of most Queensland governments which have run Queensland for all but five years of the succeeding thirty, Joh's misdemeanours seem like shoplifting lollies compared to grand larceny!

I was briefly the President of the Cairns Branch of the Liberals, but it was apparent that it was very difficult to do that job properly as a public servant, particularly in Opposition. One unusual thing did happen though. We were in the process of establishing a branch of the party in Port Douglas and a couple of politicians from southern Queensland were visiting, including Joan Sheldon. Joan was from Caloundra and we shared a few acquaintances from there. As we chatted, I confessed that although the current Liberals' state leader, Denver Beanland, seemed like a good bloke, he just did not come across as foreman material. Joan agreed and no more was said, but shortly after, I was sent to Mexico to work with the US Department of Agriculture on a disease eradication program. When I returned two months later, the Libs had a new leader—Joan Sheldon! Well, bugger me! And when Labor was finally defeated, two elections later, Joan became the State Treasurer.

The TB eradication program continued and for some reason the Normanton area was included in my division. I spent some time there as we were trying a new blood test for TB, and discovered a unique community, or communities really, because nearby was the fishing town of Karumba. Apparently, neither town was big enough by itself to support a service club so they combined to form an Apex Club and this led to the staging of the annual Snake Creek Turnout. Snake Creek is a spot on the road from Normanton to Chillagoe. There is nothing there, but the topography was suitable for making a sports arena. No doubt other events were run, but the famous events were the dog races. There was a big dog race and a little dog race. The dogs would be held at one end of the arena by various friends of the owners, and the owners would stand at the other end and call their dogs when the gun went off. It became quite a famous event, as you might expect.

Back in Karumba, there lived a couple of blokes who

liked a drink. They were probably fishermen. Everyone in Karumba is a fisherman and most of them like a drink. It seems that the local policeman used to express concern when he saw them full of beer at the local pub and would ask how they could drive home. The reply was always the same, 'Toby is driving.' Eventually, the constable discovered that Toby was a dog, so he did the only responsible thing that he could do. He took him down to the police station, photographed him, and gave him a driver's licence! This level of community engagement deserved to be recognised, and it was. Toby had a race named after him.

When I heard about what happened, I was consumed by a burning ambition. I always wanted to win the Melbourne Cup, but most people do. I also wouldn't have minded getting into the swag with Elle McPherson, but most normal blokes shared that goal as well; however, my main aim was, before I died, to have on my mantelpiece a trophy engraved with the following words:

Snake Creek Turnout
Toby Memorial
Big Dog Race
First

Of course, that was nearly thirty years ago, so I expect

Elle might be out of warranty by now, but I guess I am as well.

And my dog has died!

The Federal Government administers quarantine these days, but when I was in Cairns they used to pay the Queensland Government to do the work. Animal quarantine was looked after by the Veterinary Services Branch of DPI and plant quarantine was administered by the Agriculture Branch. There had been a 12-metre-long quarantine motor boat in Brisbane that was surplus to requirements and so it was given to the Water Police in Cairns. In exchange for this, the Water Police provided us with thirty days of free charter work per year. The idea was that we would cruise up the coast checking that international yachtsmen and women did not land and bring their rabid dogs or cats ashore. It was all a bit of a joke really, but fun to spend ten days or so getting paid to do an ocean cruise. The first time I went we got stuck in Princess Charlotte Bay for a week due to Cyclones Ernie and Mena. The offsetting factor was that we had time to land at Bathurst Head one day and help ourselves from the state's biggest colony of black-lipped oysters. I was chef that night and under the griller of the boat's little gas stove I cooked the world's biggest Oysters Kilpatrick! Fantastic! I took a photo, but it didn't do it justice.

The second quarantine cruise I did was a bit more

dramatic. We came across a couple of big motor boats anchored together on one occasion and the Police Sergeant and my Stock Inspector motored over to have a chat. The boats were owned by a couple of mates who did occasional cruises together and whenever they came across backwaters where flotsam might wash ashore, they would stop and look to see if they might find saleable articles such as old-fashioned glass fishing buoys which, apparently, were worth good money. They were relieved to see our guys and gave them their most recent find, which was brought back to our boat. It was a plastic sphere about 25cm in diameter, which pulled apart to reveal another, smaller sphere and so on. In total there were eight such spheres and in the middle of the last one was a plastic bag containing one kilogram of white powder! When the bag was opened, we gazed intently at the powder, wondering what it might be. The youngest policeman licked his finger, dipped it in the powder, then licked it again. We looked expectantly at him and the police sergeant asked, 'Well, what is it?' The young bloke replied, 'Buggered if I know. I have just seen them do that on TV.'

We anchored that night near the Aboriginal township of Lockhart River and the next day went ashore where the powder was put on a flight to Cairns for identification. It turned out to be something quite innocuous and the spheres comprised a float from a Japanese fishing boat long line.

CENTRAL AMERICA

When I had returned to Australia after my stint in Vietnam, I declared that I would never leave again. Pretty stupid really, and fortunately, I had a chance to renege on my vow while I was in Cairns. There is a blowfly in Papua New Guinea which is much more destructive than our usual ones. The screw-worm fly (SWF) physically damages tissue, while our local flies only irritate the surface (despite which they can still cause some severe reactions). Actually, there are two species of SWF which, by a process of evolutionary convergence, have developed almost identical life cycles. One, *Chrysomyia bezziana*, is in Papua New Guinea and some other places and the other, *Cochliomyia hominivorax*, is in the Americas. The second fly's name tells a story. When the Spanish invaders were trekking across South America, one man suffered a bleeding nose and lay under a tree to rest. While he did so, a fly laid its eggs in the blood around his nostrils. The eggs hatched and the larvae migrated into his nose where they drove him mad with pain as they started to eat his soft nasal tissues, hence the name, *hominivorax* (homini meaning man, and vorax meaning to eat, as in *carnivore*). Anyhow, it was decided that Australia was at risk of flies crossing Torres Strait and getting established in Cape York Peninsula, so I was sent to Central America to work with the United States Department of Agriculture (USDA) which was running an eradication program. At the time, the Minister for Primary Industries, Ed Casey, was getting a bit wary about approving overseas trips for staff as he suspected (probably correctly) that many were just junkets. While awaiting his approval, I had, coincidentally, to pick him up from Cairns airport one day and asked him about my chances. He enquired where I was going and when El Salvador was mentioned he immediately approved the trip. He reckoned going there would be no junket! Funnily enough, on many occasions when I had been to the races and lost money, I used to console myself with the observation that at least I wasn't in El Salvador!

The trip involved visits to four countries: Mexico, Guatemala, Belize and El Salvador. The Americans had a big laboratory in Tuxtla Gutierrez near the bottom of Mexico where they bred SWF and then irradiated them to make them sterile. They were then flown over the target regions and released for the sterile males to mate with wild females and produce sterile eggs. Sounds amazing and it is, and it works. They started in Texas and the plan was to gradually work south until they got to Panama where it would be relatively inexpensive to maintain a buffer zone. There was no possibility of eradication in South America. By the time of my visit, Mexico was almost clean and the program was running in Guatemala and Belize and just starting in El Salvador. One unforeseen problem that had to be countered in Mexico was that, when the fly had been eradicated, the locals working at the plant would no longer have jobs. They had to be screened when they left work to make sure no healthy flies were smuggled out to be released into the countryside!

In the time I spent in Mexico I got the impression from the Americans I worked with that they had a very low opinion of the local men; however, one of the administrators in Mexico City gave me an interesting statistic. He said that in the time he had worked in Mexico, he had known twenty-eight married Americans who had gone to Tuxtla Gutierrez and twenty-one of them had got divorced and married Mexican women.

My first port of call was Mexico City, where I met up with the people running the whole eradication program in Central America. I arrived late at night at a high-class hotel which I had been booked into by the Australian embassy.

Sorry about that! It was full. They arranged for me to be taken to another place which was perfectly comfortable, but the experience left me a bit bemused. I stayed in Mexico City for several days then and also returned there before leaving to come home. The pollution was so bad that more than a short time spent outside would make my eyes water. Notwithstanding that, the city was an amazing place. It has the world's biggest Plaza de Toros, holding 41,000 people I was told, and I shamefacedly confess that I went to a bull-fight and enjoyed the experience. You could almost smell the testosterone in the air and I imagined that the spectators all went home and screwed their brains out with both sexes fantasising that the bloke was a matador!

There is also an enormous park, Chapultapec Park, in the middle of the city. It occupies over 500ha and contains the amazing Chapultapec Castle which was built on an Aztec sacred site. If you find history boring, skip this next bit, but I found it fascinating. In 1861, France, Spain and the United Kingdom invaded Mexico after it had announced a suspension of debt repayment. The Pommies and the Spanish negotiated a deal and went home, but the French stayed and wanted to run the place. To do that, Napoleon III got Austrian Archduke Maximilian to establish a pro-French Mexican monarchy. The Yanks weren't too happy about this, but they had a civil war of their own at the time so they could not interfere. However, when that war finished the Americans supported the Mexican rebels and Maximilian's rule ended with his execution in 1867 after three years on the throne. The castle served many functions over the years, including a stint as Maximilian's residence, but is now a wonderful museum.

One Sunday in the city I was at a bit of a loose end, so I read through a tourist brochure in the hotel room. It extolled the virtues of a place called the Jardin del Arte (Garden of the Art) where artists would take their paintings, etcetera, for public display and sale every Sunday. It used to be called Sullivan Park, but I got the impression that the local Chamber of Commerce, or its Mexican equivalent, had decided to give it a sexier name. Anyhow I caught a taxi, of which Mexico City possesses about a million, all VWs, and directed my driver to the Jardin del Arte. He did not have a clue and so I thought I might have more chance using the original name, Sullivan Park. Well, Sullivan is a good old Irish name and you could not mispronounce that, could you? Still no success. After several circuits of the district, my driver spied a couple of smartly dressed young men walking along the side of the road and, surmising that one of them might speak English, he stopped and called out. He was right. They both spoke English and my problem was solved. In Spanish, the letter 'u' is pronounced 'oo', ll is pronounced 'y', and v is pronounced 'b'. Sullivan Park then becomes Soo-ya-bun Park. How simple was that? It was about 100 metres away. Travel is educational and it can also be humbling.

The whole Central American adventure was a big eye-opener for me. Guatemala was the first country where I got on-the-ground experience and that started almost as soon as I arrived in Guatemala City. The Yank in charge of the show there was complaining bitterly as a day or so before he had been robbed at gunpoint in a car park when he went to buy a pizza. His main complaint seemed to be that, not only had his wallet been stolen, the bastards took his pizza as well!

Before leaving Cairns, I had spent several months teaching myself Spanish with a Charles Berlitz tape. I had got the phrases and pronunciation pretty well learned, but, of course, could not hold a proper conversation. I was also not aware that some of the content of the tape was fairly dated. The usual statement one made on being introduced was *mucho gusto en conocerte*, meaning pleased to meet you, or a shortened version *mucho gusto*. According to Berlitz, there were other ways. When I first went into the Guatemala SWF Program office, I saw one of the most beautiful women I have ever encountered, even though she was about eight-and-a-half months pregnant! On being introduced, I recalled a gracious statement which Berlitz had said was an alternative greeting. I said, 'A *sus pies*', which literally means 'at your feet'. The men all shrieked with mirth and said things like, 'You'll get on, you sneaky prick', while the woman blushed! Apparently, that form of address hadn't been used in normal conversation since about 1850!

Funny things happen in Central America. The USDA liked to engage local contractors for the SWF distribution. They were supposed to fly grids and release a box of flies for every square mile they covered. Apparently, one of the contractors flew off and was eventually forced down in Nicaragua, not even a neighbouring country! It was not known if he was trading drugs or guns or what! Three Yanks and I drove to the east coast town of Puerto Barrios, the town the plane had left from, to investigate. On the way, we took a diversion to a small town a short way south-east of the main road. There was nobody around, but under a very big tree like a Moreton Bay Fig, were about twenty ponies, all saddled and tethered. In the distance we could see the top of a mountain range which was the border with Honduras. If you live in a country like Nicaragua, it is hard to amass much internationally tradeable wealth, as there is no demand for the local currency. One way out of the problem is to get some cattle and drive them towards the USA. The closer they get to America, the more they are worth as the Yanks buy them with US dollars and put them in feed lots. Of course, crossing borders poses a problem. This is overcome by bribing border guards and when that has been accomplished, the team of horsemen is notified and they ride up and take over the droving. Our guys were not all that worried about the illegal traffic; their problem was that the cattle came from places where the SWF were prevalent and could reinfest clean areas further north.

I went from Guatemala to Belize and that was a major change. It is very low lying and very humid and tropical. The main city, Belize City, was devastated by Hurricane Hattie in 1961 and the British, who were still in charge then (when it was called British Honduras), moved the capital inland to Belmopan—a bit like Canberra, but only a very tiny bit. Belize City is a most unlovely place and I was told that, unlike most hurricanes, Hurricane Hattie actually did $7 million worth of good! For the first week or so, I stayed in Belmopan, at the Bullfrog Inn, where I asked the manager what time breakfast was available. He replied that the girls were there any time after 6.30am, so I turned up at 6.30am. Silly me! When he said 'any time', he meant any time. Some days they did not arrive until 8 o'clock! I also spent a week travelling around with a young bloke called Omar checking the SWF targets, sheep that had small cuts to attract the flies. We found none, but I did learn that

Omar's father was a retired Chicle Tapper. You don't run across a lot of them these days. Chicle is the sap from the Sapodilla tree which was used for making chewing gum. A synthetic product is used these days. I tried at one stage to cross the border back into Guatemala so I could visit the Mayan site, Tikal, but was turned back at the border because I had only a single-entry visa. I actually expected that I would just bribe the guards and get through, but no such luck. When he saw my disappointment, Omar took me to a Belizian temple/pyramid. It was open to the public and quite impressive, but one old caretaker and we two were the only ones there. Omar also showed me another temple right next to San Ignacio, the town where I was staying at that time. It was also fairly impressive, but quite overgrown. Omar told me how he and his mates used to play there when he was a kid. I read years later how a group of amateur archaeologists from Canada had discovered it and were returning in their annual holidays to open it up.

The last country I went to was El Salvador, and it was the one I liked the most, despite possible danger from rebels when I was away from the populated centres. Happily, I never encountered any.

Despite its political uncertainty, the locals I spent time with seemed to be optimistic and hardworking and the local taxis were the only ones I saw in Central America with two-way radios. The countryside is quite hilly and erosion is widespread where hillsides have been cleared for corn planting. There are no contour banks and rain removes the topsoil after a couple of seasons. Overall, though, El Salvador is very fertile, carrying 1.2 million cattle to feed 6 million people in a country only twice as big as Bulloo Downs!

A new system of handling the sterile flies was being developed in El Salvador. Previously, the flies would be hatched out in Mexico, then transported to the various airfields from which they would be released. In El Salvador it was decided to transport the pupae and hatch them out in San Salvador, the nation's capital. The site for this exercise was the original airport, which was in the middle of the city. It had become too small and a bigger, better, commercial one was established several kilometres out of town, so the military had taken over the old one. The SWF facility occupied a small section of this. Each day as we arrived and left, we would pass through a military check-point so the guards became quite familiar with us. However, on one occasion a new guard was on duty. He did not know who we were and was inclined to subject us to intense scrutiny. At this stage I should tell you the name for screw-worm fly in Spanish. It is *Gusano barrenador del ganado*, which literally means 'maggot burrowing of livestock.' You will probably be familiar with the Spanish term for horseman, *caballero,* and the term for cattleman, *vaquero.* Well now there is a new one. The new guard was told by one of his mates that we were okay because we were Gusaneros! Maggot cowboys!

The reason I was sent to Central America was to learn enough to be able to contribute to a national strategy for controlling a possible SWF incursion. I did what was asked, but in truth could not convince myself that Australia was seriously threatened. SWF thrives in proper rainforest, but Cape York Peninsula has almost none. There is a bit at the top, but it is not typical rainforest. There is no understorey and it gets very dry in the dry season. I suspect that any larva trying to pupate in that environment would die from dehydration either before or shortly after emerging. Overall, though, it was a wonderful experience and convinced me to put foreign travel back on the agenda.

NATURAL RESOURCE MANAGEMENT

The defeat of the Bjelke-Petersen government led to major changes to the way many Queensland government departments were administered. One way was that there were many more 'workshops' designed to make us better managers or problem solvers, or whatever. One of these workshops was held in Cairns and my counterpart from Townsville, John Roberts, attended and he and his wife, Margie, stayed with us for the duration. This was a lot of fun and involved excess grog consumption every night they were there. One night our son, Sam, told us about his homework, which had involved pretending to be a World War I soldier at the Somme writing a letter home. In our alcohol-fuelled enthusiasm, John and I decided that an aura of authenticity might be added if we took the letter out into the backyard and fired a bullet through it. My semi-automatic .22 had fired countless rounds over the years when left on the farm after I went away to school and uni, but I had not actually used it for ages. Had I tried, I would have discovered that the firing pin was so worn that it would not detonate a round. We had a couple of attempts, but the gun would not go off. Thank heavens! We lived in the middle of a densely-populated suburb.

I guess I can be thankful that the eras of inclusiveness and gender irrelevance and black lives mattering had not yet arrived, but there still seemed to be endless meetings. The proposed change in the way that regions were going to operate seemed like bullshit to me and I had a lot of trouble keeping my mouth shut, so it became obvious that the time had come to move on. The opportunity arose to become the Executive Officer of the Queensland Landcare Council and the Queensland Catchment Management Coordinating Committee and so I took it, meaning we had to move to Brisbane. The job sounded like it might be really interesting, but it wasn't. I was just a secretary and so that couldn't last, so after a year or so I then became the Manager of Catchment Management in the Queensland section of the Murray-Darling Basin, based in Toowoomba. You might think that Flora would have been getting a bit sick of moving all the time by now and you would probably be right.

This new job was a bit better, but there were still problems. The Federal Government had enthusiastically introduced Landcare and provided lots of money for various community projects. The cunning trick, though, was that the State Government insisted on being involved in many of the projects, thus providing a way to milk the Fed's money to pay State wages. This, of course, meant that there was less available for the community groups. I predicted that this would eventually lead to a loss of community enthusiasm, and I was right.

* * *

It was not all bad news though, because when the election was held in 1995, the Liberal/National Coalition surprised even themselves and won, and because of my various experiences, I became the Senior Policy Advisor to the Minister for Natural Resources, Howard Hobbs! That was a terrific job and I was very sad that the Borbidge government only lasted one term. Some of the best events were the Ministerial Council meetings, where the ministers from all states, who had similar portfolios, would get together once a year to discuss, and no doubt decide the fate of, various issues. On one occasion the topic was the recent introduction of Calicivirus to combat the rabbit plague. This was interesting because while I was in Mexico there was a national campaign to eradicate that virus. Apparently, a Mexican returning from China had brought the disease back with him (does that ring a bell?) and the only way to eradicate it was to kill all rabbits. This was a problem because many Mexican families bred rabbits as a dietary protein source. The government had to get rid of all of them and then replace them when the eradication program was completed. Back in Australia, *Myxomatosis* was losing its potency and a new control measure was proposed. It was envisaged that the Calicivirus should be cultured on Kangaroo Island until there was enough for it to be released on the mainland over as wide an area as possible in a short time. Unfortunately, someone managed to get hold of some samples and released them early. Apparently, it was highly contagious, so dead rabbits could be taken to clean areas with large rabbit populations and the disease would break out and spread quite quickly. John Anderson, the Deputy Prime Minister, was chairman of this meeting and was asked how quickly the virus spread. He replied, 'About 100 km/h on bitumen roads and a bit slower on dirt.'

I guess the highlight of the job was the time that I accompanied the Minister, Howard Hobbs, on a tour with the Queensland Timber Board to look at sustainable forestry management in various other countries— USA, Canada, England, Scotland and Sweden. It was a dirty job, but someone had to do it. And the best part of the tour was the time spent being guided by scientist Patrick Moore in British Columbia, especially on Vancouver Island. Moore was one of the three Canadian scientists who started Greenpeace and he had resigned after it was taken over by a group of European extremists. He was a good bloke and an excellent guide with an amazing depth of knowledge. We had brought the Queensland head of the Rainforest Protection Society, Aila Ketoe, with us in an attempt to show her the real world and Patrick managed to dispel most of the misconceptions she laboured under. Unfortunately, it did not last and when she returned to her home base, she reverted to type managing after Labor won the next election, to convince new Premier, Peter Beattie, to lock up the native forests, despite them being logged quite sustainably for 100 years or so.

My time as Senior Ministerial Policy Advisor actually did not last until the election. The Minister was severely criticised by his wife, with considerable justification, for taking his electorate secretary on the Timber Board trip, and it went public. Parliament shuts down from Christmas until school goes back at the end of January and Flora and I went to the USA to visit our daughter and her family. On returning, I was contacted by the Minister and advised that his wife had 'spat the dummy'. He said she had been interviewed by a reporter from the *Sunday Mail*, Queensland's only Sunday newspaper. Howard said he expected the report to be a minor one, perhaps on page ten or twelve. Well! Sorry about that! It occupied just about the whole front page!

The inevitable consequence was that the boss lost his job and so I lost mine. I had been seconded from the public service and was due to go back there; however, people with my history are a bit hard to place, so it was probably a relief to all when I was given a redundancy. Howard Hobbs had been told he would get a ministry if the government was re-elected and I was confident I would get my old job back when that happened. Unfortunately, the voters had other ideas. Pauline Hansen's One Nation Party emerged in spectacular fashion and that was the end of the Coalition Government, my job hopes, and responsible financial management for Queensland.

ENGLAND

I was fifty-three years old without a job and the idea of going back to private practice had no appeal at all, so when the Mad Cow Disease occurred in the UK and they were desperate to have more vets in their meatworks, I went to England. It was a pretty mediocre job, but it gave me English £s and a chance to explore over there. Flora followed after I had done some initial training and we ended up in Bedford, about an hour by train north of London.

The Meat Hygiene Service required vets to conduct ante-mortem inspection of the livestock and ensure best hygiene practice was followed when the carcasses were processed. This did not only happen at big abattoirs, but also at small slaughterhouses run by local butchers. On a Monday, a town butcher might kill five cattle, forty sheep, five goats and six pigs, this being what he would sell for the week. They would usually need a Meat Inspector to attend for the whole time and a Vet would only come for an hour to check hygiene and fill out forms. It was as boring as it sounds, but did allow me to see the countryside. I might visit seven or eight such places every week and through one of them I learned a very interesting lesson about Pommie class distinction. As an Aussie, I never thought about class distinction, believing it was a relic of a bygone era, but to my surprise, I detected evidence of it in lots of aspects of English life. Having a Meat Inspector attend a small country slaughterhouse for a whole day's operation is an expensive exercise and can be avoided under special circumstances. If a butcher is sufficiently trustworthy, he can keep the organs that the inspector must examine in such a way that the carcass can be correlated in the event of disease being detected. This might mean an inspector need only attend for one hour instead of seven or eight. There was only one place where this happened. Coincidentally, the proprietor used to always be referred to as Mr Morris, whereas all others would be Fred or Jack or such. One day, when I was in the big abattoir that was my base, I asked all the inspectors during smoko why Mr Morris was always called Mr Morris. Perhaps the sharpest of them, a bloke from a very low socio-economic background who had worked his way up from the slaughter floor to become an Inspector, replied, 'He's a gentleman.' I couldn't believe my ears. He then went on to say, 'He's got his own shoot.' For the uninitiated, this would be a patch of scrub, perhaps four hectares, where pheasants (reared for the purpose) would be released so they could be shot by the owner and his friends assembled for a day's outing. I'm sure it is great fun and Mr Morris actually invited me to come one time, but unfortunately, I could not make it. I hasten to add that he was a thoroughly decent bloke and quite unpretentious.

One of the jobs the vets had to do was a monthly hygiene assessment of the premises. Various aspects would be given scores which, in the ideal case, would add up to 100. The whole thing was a bit of a joke really and a meeting would be attended by relevant staff to discuss why an 87 score had been downgraded to 86. One small slaughterhouse I had to work in was probably the worst in England, if not the whole world. Maintaining the illusion of strictness that seemed to be required, I persisted with fluctuating scores in the low 80s which seemed to have been the norm for long before my time. Apparently, the Meat Hygiene Service Directors felt the vets in general had not been nearly strict enough with our assessments, so we were all required to attend a weekend workshop (unpaid) to learn how to do them properly. When it was time for the 'hell hole' to be assessed again, I scored it at 38! Bottom line is, I never went there again. That made the wasted weekend all worthwhile!

Although I usually only worked there on weekends, my

notional base was at a fairly large plant, Dawn Cardington, on the outskirts of Bedford. On one occasion I was there mid-week and found myself in the smoko room with one of the Meat Inspectors, a Ghanaian named Kwabina, which is one of those African words which means 'born on Tuesday', or 'third son', or something like that. The other inspectors called him Ken! He was a very decent, conservative type of bloke and still identified with his community (I resist the impulse to say tribe) and intended to return to Ghana when he retired. In an attempt to draw him out, I made a comparison between the convicts who had been sent to Australia and the Negro slaves sent to the Americas. I said that the current descendants of those convicts now often visited England and maintained a robust, friendly relationship with the locals. I then asked how he felt about the African Americans coming across to the UK. Before his politically correct gears could engage, he said, with a rising inflection, 'They're slaves!' He quickly went on to add, 'I know now that what we did was wrong, but back then it was just business.' It may come as a surprise to some that the horrible white men did not land and muster up mobs of unfortunate natives to sell as slaves in the New World—the unfortunate natives had already been mustered up by their countrymen. Their attitude seemed to be that if you were stupid enough or weak enough to be caught, you basically got what you deserved.

Kwabina seemed to me to be the only inspector who read the *Times* newspaper. Everyone else read the *Sun*, which was famous for its page three scantily-clad girls, editorial policy of a salacious inclination and clever headlines. On one occasion it published a list of what were considered to be the best of these. I will never forget two of them. One related to a woman, Amanda, who had got a bit carried away after filling up on the free grog in Business Class on a flight from New York to London. Apparently, she and her male co-traveller, whom she had never met before, were sprung having it away under an airline blanket in one of the seats, leading to the headline, Mile High Mandy gets Randy on Brandy! The second memorable offering related to a policeman who had a sex change. There had apparently been much discussion about whether he would be able to seamlessly become a policewoman. Fortunately for him/her, it was allowed, and the *Sun* published gleefully, No Knobby Bobby Keeps Jobbie!

Living in Bedford was hardly thrilling, but it did have its moments. We regularly took pub walks on Sundays. There was a booklet listing the best walks and the appropriate pubs to repair to for lunch when the three or four miles of the suggested walk had been covered. Ploughman's Lunch was our favourite and I still dream about the Stilton cheese which was always included. On a recent trip to the UK, I asked a publican about the apparent lack of Ploughman's Lunches on pub menus these days and he told me there was no demand any more. My God! If they can maintain the Monarchy, surely they can maintain Ploughman's Lunches! They are far more important.

The other thing I enjoyed in Bedford was the Folk Club. It used to meet every Thursday night in an upstairs room of the Fleur de Lis Hotel. Perhaps a dozen or so enthusiasts would attend and we just went around the room with each person in turn singing a song. We might get perhaps three goes per person. A couple of the singers were very good and the rest were a fairly mixed bunch, but I made some interesting discoveries about Pommies while I was at the Folk Club meetings. One was that they really had very little time for the Irish, including Irish music. I had a favourite Clancy Brothers song which made reference to a place called Bearna Baol, but I never had a clue where or what it was. Thinking that the English might enlighten me, I foolishly asked if anyone knew about it. Total blank stares linked with a hint of suspicion were the response. I also discovered they weren't all that fussed about poetry, or not about my new poem anyhow, when I gave them its first public reading:

Daffodils

I wandered, lonely as a wombat,
so depressed I groaned aloud.
Gazed into the azure heavens, boring, not a single cloud.
Saw a million flowers blooming,
up and down the dales and hills.
Every fucking one was yellow. God I'm sick of daffodils!

Strangely enough, that wasn't really greeted with rapturous applause. Perhaps they prefer blank verse.

The most disappointing failure of our time there was missing the Joan Baez concert. One of the folk club women arrived one night to say how wonderful it had been when Joan Baez sang in a concert at Northampton, just a short drive north of Bedford on the previous weekend. She then told me that Joan was going to sing at the Corn Exchange in Cambridge the following Saturday night. I immediately contacted the Corn Exchange to find I could get tickets and, of course, was advised that the concert was sold out. Like a dickhead, I thought, *Well, that's the end of that.* Surely, if we had gone, we would have been able to sit on the steps or something. Anyhow, there are not many actions I have taken over the years that I regret years later, despite many of them not having been anything to brag about, but I regret not having tried harder to see and hear Joan Baez. If you ever get to Goomboorian, Joanie, please look us up. I've got a pretty good guitar I can lend you.

I had gone to England at the end of October 1998, and had to put in five or six weeks of training to become an Official Veterinary Surgeon (OVS) of the Meat Hygiene Service (MHS). For decades past, the ante-mortem inspection of animals scheduled to be slaughtered at various country slaughterhouses attached to the butcher shops had been carried out by the local vets. When the system changed and was 'upgraded' there was a call for tenders to be submitted from vets wanting to do the work. I suspect that most local vets regarded this as their divine right and tendered quite high quotes. A couple of enterprising young blokes who had a practice in the Midlands challenged the system and ended up with contracts for the MHS work in slaughterhouses and abattoirs all over the UK. When I arrived, they had 70 vets working for them and by the time I left it was more like 140! Pommies did not want to do the work, and I do not blame them, but the Spaniards flocked in. Spanish Veterinary Science degrees were rated as the equivalent standard to the British ones under the rules of the European Union, but they were not. The clinical expertise of the Spanish was sadly lacking, but they did have lots of training in the fields of bureaucratic oversight. Therefore, they were well placed to do MHS work. Most of the ones I worked with were really nice people, even to the extent of including in their social gatherings other Spaniards whom they did not like very much. One young man whom I shared training with (I was linked to him because he had a car and we had to travel around to several abattoirs) was named Joaquim Menzinger. A lovely bloke, whose father must have been German. You may not be aware, but Joaquim gets shortened to Quim. Qu in Spanish is pronounced, as it often is in English, as 'K'. So, Quim is 'Kim'. But there is a problem. Quim in English is often pronounced 'kwim', and is a slang term meaning vulva. Quim wrote his name on the front of his notebook, and I hastened to urge him to write it in the English way! He could see my point.

Quite a number of the Spaniards came to work in England as a way of improving their English language skills. It continues to baffle me that white English-speaking males (mostly) all over the world seem to be accepting vilification for what they are while the rest of the world really wants to be like them!

Quim had actually come to Scotland and completed a Master's degree at Aberdeen University the previous year, basically to improve his English. He did not really care what the course was. After we completed our OVS training, we were then sent off to various places all over the country to work. Quim was posted to Perth in Scotland, but he and a mate rented a flat in Edinburgh and he used to drive an hour to work. All meatworks shut for four days at Easter, so during the brief holiday we drove up to visit him. Naturally, much grog was consumed in the night of our arrival, so after our big drive Flora and I went to bed earlier than the locals—a bed kindly vacated for us by Quim. The generosity of his sacrifice was fully appreciated the next morning when we saw him sleeping fully-clothed on the hard floor beside us, using my shoes and socks as a pillow!

The English bureaucracy is an amazing institution. After I had been working for the MHS for nine months or so, I decided that I would try to get a different job. The problem with abattoirs was that you always had to be there when they were working, so I could never leave early on Friday or arrive late on Monday to get more value out of a weekend. I therefore decided to apply for a Government Vet job. The country was divided into about twenty-two regions and each one needed a Government Vet. The Government had difficulty filling the positions because much more money could be made in private practice and, on this occasion, there were five vacancies. I applied and nothing happened for some time. Flora's sister had arrived from Australia for a visit and we had arranged to go to France for a week in September. Flora's English cousin and her husband owned a holiday house in the rural village of St Benoit, a couple of hours drive south of Paris and they had kindly offered it to us. Shortly before we were due to leave, I got a call from the Government job people telling me I had to turn up on Wednesday of the following week for an interview. I said I could not make it, but if the interview could be delayed until Friday, I could return from France early. This was totally out of the question for them so that was the end of it. A few weeks later, I contacted the job people to find out the situation and was advised that three of the five positions had been filled. I then wondered if there might be a second round of interviews, but was advised that the next round would be in a year's time. So there, dickhead colonial!

St Benoit was an interesting place, completely off the tourist-beaten path, and I think we were the only non-locals in town. An enterprising real estate agent took the liberty of dropping a brochure in our mail box and it was quite educational. Paris is Paris, so one expects Paris Real Estate to be horrendously expensive, but rural France is a different kettle of fish completely. One could buy a 'house', and I use the term in its very loosest sense, for as little as £10,000. It would have no power, nor water, nor services and be in a pretty sad condition, but it would be a place one could use as a base. Double that price might get something habitable.

That was in 1999 and I understand that prices have risen since, but are still very reasonable provided they are rural.

While we were in France, we drove south one day towards Limoges, to the ruined village of Oradour-sur-Glane. Just by chance I had seen an article about it in the house where we were staying and I was fascinated. In mid-1944, the Allies were moving up from the Mediterranean and the Nazis looked to be in big trouble. The French Resistance had been doing annoying damage in the region and it seemed that one of the Nazi leaders decided to severely punish the locals before retreating north. All inhabitants of the village were rounded up, the men and boys taken to one area and killed and the women and children taken to the church and killed. There were a few survivors, but 642 people lost their lives. In an attempt, I suppose, to hide the evidence from the approaching Allies, the whole village was subsequently burned. After the war ended, President de Gaulle decreed that the village would not be rebuilt. It would be left as it was and be maintained as a permanent memorial. I am so glad he made that decision. It was a very sobering experience to walk through the ruins, but nobody regretted the visit.

Each of the British regions which did not get a vet (because not enough had applied for the jobs) were able to employ a contract vet until a permanent one could be found, so I explored that option, thinking if I worked as a contractor for a year then it would be easy to get a full-time job in the next round of appointments. I went to Ayr for an interview and was offered a position there. However, before the time came to get out of the meatworks job and move to Ayr, a bolt came out of the blue.

One of the Stock Inspectors whom I used to oversee in Western Queensland had worked hard and upgraded his qualifications and had become a Regional Manager for the Department of Agriculture in Western Australia. He turned up in the UK, leading a group of farmers and graziers on a study tour, or something—taxpayer funded of course. We got on the booze one night in London and he urged me to come back to Australia and go to Western Australia and work for him. I was still in abattoirs at the time, so the idea was quite attractive and that is what I did. As you can imagine, Flora was delighted at the prospect of another major move!

We didn't leave England straight away and I had a couple of interesting experiences before we did go. Via a company called British Horseracing Abroad I attended the 1999 running of the famous French horse race, the Prix de l'Arc de Triomphe at Longchamps. It was a one-day excursion, flying out of Heathrow Airport early on a Sunday morning and arriving back at about 10.30pm the same day, in time for me to get home at midnight. My plan had been to catch the train from Bedford to Kings Cross, then another to the airport. Ha, ha! I waited at the station and watched the train I thought I was catching roll on through—the station wasn't even open! Plan B was then implemented and I hurriedly drove down to London. Fortunately, it all worked out okay and Montjeu beat a visiting Japanese horse in the Arc, though the track was so wet that the racing was a bit boring.

Shortly before leaving, we realised that there were a couple of relatively close places that we had not seen, so we visited Devon and Cornwall one weekend, resisting the temptation to get lost in the Dartmoor mists, and then went to Wales during the Christmas break. This latter excursion found us, on a Sunday morning, in a place that only the Welsh could name—Mumbles. Never heard of it, but it had two important features. One, was that it was the home of excellent Welsh pop singer, and not a bad sort, Bonnie Tyler. Two, was that according to the local newspaper, Bonnie was being visited by the world's absolutely most beautiful sheila, Catherine Zeta-Jones. Unfortunately, she missed me!

Talking about Mumbles reminds me of a funny experience I had walking down George Street in Brisbane one day with a female workmate. Approaching us from the opposite direction was a moderately overweight woman in very tight stretch pants—a bit like tracksuit pants. My friend said something about mumble pants. I asked, 'Why do you call them mumble pants?' and she replied, 'You can see the lips move, but you can't hear what they are saying!'

Driving home from Wales took us through the Brecon Beacons National Park, a beautiful place. Flora wanted to stop the car and go for a walk. As I was suffering badly from some exotic 'flu' which the Pommies had blamed on the visiting (victorious) Aussie rugby team, and it was actually snowing at the time, I refused to stop the car. I figured she must have had a secret insurance policy on me because she whinged for miles! Walking in the snow would have killed me!

The Aussie rugby team had just won the Rugby World Cup, which had brought me much glee for a reason much more mundane and widespread than national pride—greed! Australia beat Wales in the first semi-final, and France (in the best game of rugby I have ever seen) beat the New Zealand All Blacks in the other one. Reasoning that lightning never strikes twice in the same place, I went to Ladbrokes, the bookmakers, and asked what odds I could get for Australia to beat France by more than 20 points. They informed me that the system does not work like that. I had to name the margin spread. Eventually, I had £10 at 16-1 for Australia to win by between 21 and 25 points, and another £10 at 20-1 for the Aussies to win by between

26 and 30. Australia won by 23 points! If Tim Horan had kicked another field goal it would have been worth £40 to me!

WESTERN AUSTRALIA

We left England right after New Year and ended up in Perth, WA, in late January for a week or so's induction. Perth is quite a nice place but is in a bit of a time warp. With daylight saving in most eastern states, but not in WA which is already two hours behind, one had to get up quite early to have a bet on the Randwick or Flemington races.

During the induction I had to fly up to Carnarvon for a day. This was where I was to be based for my job as Regional Manager of Industry Development in the Southern Rangelands. I had to sneak that in somehow—it sounds quite impressive! Leaving the plane at Carnarvon airport, I was stunned by the heat. I know my tolerance might have been weakened by the time spent in the UK, but 47 degrees!

Carnarvon is an unusual place. North of it there is summer rainfall and south has winter rain. In a good year the northern rain might come south to Carnarvon and the southern rain might go north. In a bad year, neither climatic norm happens. That was my year. In the twelve months I was there, it rained on one day, and I was in Perth at the time.

My position was funded under a joint State/Federal government initiative called the Gascoyne Murchison Strategy (GMS). The Gascoyne and Murchison Rivers drain the area roughly east from Carnarvon and Geraldton. A study had been done which indicated that the local sheep grazing community was in big trouble. In fact, despite having no employees and doing no major maintenance, a representative group of producers surveyed in the Meekatharra area needed wool prices to rise by 25 percent to achieve break-even. The average property was 100,000ha and carried 10,000 dry sheep equivalents (ie. castrated males, called wethers). There are about 200 such places, though a few more fortunate properties had some Buffel grass and could run cattle. The GMS budget was $40m. It seemed to me they could have bought most of the struggling places with that money.

My job was to try and develop a quality assurance/regional branding system for the local producers. To this end, I enlisted the help of auditors of various quality assurance (QA) programs to identify relevant criteria. One system which got regular mention was ISO. That was the International Standards Organisation devised by the European Union. When free trade between EU countries was allowed, its aim was to develop standards so that, for example, a widget made in Italy would be of the same quality as one made in Belgium. That is all well and good, but things can get a bit overdone. I took an Auditor to a property north of Carnarvon to get an idea of what performance standards might be needed in our region. This was a place of several hundred square kilometres, fairly sandy soil, and as flat as a biscuit. The Auditor took one look at the fuel drums beside the station's small aeroplane and said, 'Well, you'll have to put a bund around that!' I can understand that in Berlin a fuel spill might get into the drains and end up in a watercourse, but here? This country is so flat that the few creeks that do exist peter out without reaching the sea. That is why Ningaloo Reef is such a marvellous place. Coral does not like fresh water, which is why the Great Barrier Reef is well offshore, but in this region there is almost no runoff, so the coral grows right up to the beach. Fuel from a broken drum would be lucky to get to 3 metres before soaking into the ground.

We also looked at the possibility of going organic, though it was a dream, really. Organic means no nasty pesticides, and no nasty pesticide means lots of dying flyblown sheep. As it is, they lose enough sheep there from flies because, at a stocking rate of one sheep per 10ha, they do not get mustered very often apart from shearing time. There is almost no grass, just shrubs, so even locating the sheep can be difficult.

There was a visit by a bloke from Marks and Spencer in the UK which caused a bit of excitement for a while. Unfortunately, the group of potential organic wool growers said to the M&S man, 'Tell us what you will pay and we will tell you if we will do it,' to which he replied, 'You show us the wool and we will tell you what we might pay.' That was the end of that dream.

I did have an idea that I thought might benefit one group of graziers, a bunch of blokes who fattened sheep on the Nullarbor Plain. I thought it was a desert, but there you go! There is underground water, but not much, so each bore must be carefully managed and not expected to water too many sheep. The issue these producers had was that they could buy weaner lambs and fatten them, but not before their first permanent teeth erupted. That meant they were no longer classed as lambs. They became hoggets. What a terrible name. Unless you were familiar with them, you might be reluctant to eat something with a name that sounds like it might be crossed with a pig. Despite the name, I am sure that I am not the only person who prefers hogget to lamb because they are bigger, just as flavoursome, and cheaper. My bright idea was that the name 'hogget' should be changed to 'two-tooth lamb', greatly advantaging the Nullarbor growers. Genius! Not all that easy though. For such a change to be made, it must be agreed to by the Ministers for Agriculture of all of the different states. I fell at the first jump! The WA Minister for Agriculture represented an electorate containing lots of traditional lamb producers so my bright idea did not even get to his desk!

Twenty years later, as I write this, I saw just the other day that the definition of 'lamb' has been changed to include animals with their first permanent teeth erupted but not fully 'in wear'. This uses the same definition that New Zealand has used for decades and was long overdue. It is not quite what I wanted, but better than nothing. I hope it helps the Nullarbor men.

In July, Flora's sister and her husband came to visit, so we took a couple of days off and went to Coral Bay. It is only a very small place with one hotel, but there is a campground with a few basic accommodation units as well, directly opposite the beach. You could walk 30m to the water and another ten to be amongst coral! Amazing! We hired one of the units, moved our gear in, and then headed off to try and catch a fish before dark. We drove several kilometres north and got our lines in, but without any success. As we started home, I discovered that the sand dunes were a problem. I had a Nissan 4WD, but in reality had absolutely zero experience driving in sand. I was aware that one should deflate the tyres, but had no idea how much air to let out and no tyre gauge either. I was buggering around letting out about one pound of pressure at a time and getting nowhere when, over the biggest dune, came a bloke with a shovel in one hand and a tyre gauge in the other! I think he had been waiting there all day in the hope of rescuing someone in distress. Funny thing was, he came from Tara, a Queensland town not far from Chinchilla where I was born. We had both come a long way. At this stage, Flora and her sister, Rosslyn, were well past being damsels, but we were certainly in distress, so he solved our problem in no time and back to Coral Bay we drove, albeit on very flat tyres.

Later that night, after we had been asleep for a few hours, there was a knock on the door. A representative of the State Emergency Service (SES) was there and he told us we needed to evacuate. There had been an earthquake near the Cocos Islands and there was the risk of a tidal wave hitting Coral Bay. Of course, our inclination was to say, 'Yeah, that'd be right,' and go back to sleep, but then thought how stupid we would be if the wave did hit and we had ignored the warning. So, we got into the Nissan and drove to a small ridge behind the campground and stayed there until about 3am when the message came through that the danger had passed. Next day we heard that the local SES boss, for whom English was a second language, had a bit of trouble translating the message from English via his native language and Japanese back into English and had issued the warning that Coral Bay was in danger of being inundated by a giant salami!

In the middle of the year, Eric Bogle came to Carnarvon on one of those Arts Council-sponsored tours. It was a bit of a shame really because shortly before, John Williamson had come and performed to a packed hall, but Eric drew only a very small crowd. I shall now tell you my Eric Bogle story. Readers may not be aware—I certainly wasn't—that the Danish Education Department has a novel way of teaching English. Each year they choose a different country where English is the official language and concentrate on different aspects of the place and Australia had been chosen for the following year. A friend of one of the Bedford Folk Club members was commissioned to record Australian songs and he contacted me to see if I would sing a couple for him. Of course, I agreed and he asked if I knew 'The Band Played Waltzing Matilda'. I told him that not only did I know it, but I regarded it as one of the greatest songs of all time. He then startled me by saying that he could get Eric Bogle's version, but as I was an Aussie, he would rather get mine. He could get Eric but he preferred me! I suggested that I might dine out on that. After the Carnarvon concert was over, Eric stayed in the lobby selling his CDs. I approached, bought one, then asked if he wanted to hear my Eric Bogle story. He replied, 'Only if it reflects well on me.'

But I told him anyway.

After a few more months of basically marking time, I was becoming a bit disillusioned in the Carnarvon job. I had been liaising with a smart, young woman from the Environment Department in Perth who was at risk of being declared redundant, so I felt no guilt at resigning and leaving her to finish my task. I had seen a position advertised in Queensland, which I believed was ideal for me, and we left in February 2001 to arrive back in Brisbane in time for my interview. Unfortunately, the job was one of those ones manufactured occasionally to allow a pay increase for an existing employee by rebranding the position at a different salary scale. Two people were interviewed and I came second. Oh, well! That's the breaks. Fortunately for me, at this time, England got an outbreak of Foot and Mouth Disease (FMD) and life took a major turn.

FOOT AND MOUTH

At the beginning of the outbreak, the British Ministry of Agriculture, Forestry and Fisheries (MAFF) sought veterinarians to come and help with the eradication campaign, but they made the mistake of offering the same pay as their regular vets. Nobody came, so the ante was upped. The new wage was £250 per day and this was very attractive at a time when A, I needed a job, and B, the exchange rate was about English 34p to the Aussie dollar. The potential negative was that there was no guarantee of how much work one might get. In the end I decided that it would be worthwhile going even if I only got a couple of weeks' work, so I went in May. As it turned out, there was no problem getting as much work as I wanted, usually seven days per week, and they also provided accommodation, a car, and £20 extra per day to buy meals! Bugger me! I stayed until late September and could have probably stayed until March the following year, but was missing Flora and couldn't talk her into coming over. She could easily have got a work permit as she had a British grannie.

On the subject of the British Ministry of Agriculture, Fisheries and Forestry, the British Prime Minister at the time, Tony Blair, was seriously dismayed by the apparent incompetence of MAFF in the early diagnosis and control of the FMD outbreak. His solution was to change its name to the Department of Environment, Food and Rural Affairs (DEFRA). Yep. That should do it!

The day after I arrived, a good mate of mine also turned up. John Walthall and I had gone through uni together as mentioned earlier and he had also been my boss at one stage when I worked in the Queensland DPI. We were accommodated at a Travel Lodge on the outskirts of Newcastle at a place called Seaton Burn and stayed there for a couple of months. We both had a break in July and, on returning, moved into a pub in the middle of Newcastle.

Many of the British pubs had a wonderful innovation which, with a bit of luck, might one day make it into Australia. On the wall behind the bar was a screen perhaps 2m wide and 40cm high. It was divided into five segments and each one contained a possible prize. The customer who had just bought a beer would be given a 'gun' and a white ball would move back and forwards across the screen. The aim was to stop the ball in one of the segments with a good prize, such as free pint, two for one, one pound pint, or a fourth I cannot recall. There was only one segment with no useful prize. What John and I discovered was that it was not just lucky chance and we got quite good at the game. The outcome was that on almost every evening, I would buy a couple of pints of Guinness, John would buy a couple of pints of Guinness, and we would have a third, either free or cheap. Then we went round the corner to an Italian restaurant and had half a litre of wine with dinner before repairing to our beds, tired but happy. I don't really wish for a recurrence of FMD but ... if required ...

This is an appropriate time to give Newcastle a plug. When first told that was where I was going to be sent to work, I confess I was a bit dismayed. I was thinking industrial revolution and little match girls dying of exposure. How wrong can you be? Newcastle is a wonderful place. The people are great, the surrounding countryside is spectacularly beautiful, and The Angel of the North, which I drove past on most days, is the world's most wonderful statue.

I was also surprised to learn that Newcastle was rated one of the world's ten best party cities. The main reason was that it is a relatively short flight from Scandinavia, and grog is so expensive in those countries, that if, say, a bunch of Norwegians want to have a buck's party, they will take a plane to Newcastle and have it there. Along the river, the area called Quayside, there are heaps of restaurants and bars and, for some reason that I could never fathom, the local girls paraded along there in the skimpiest clothing, even in cold weather. Perhaps that is another of the attractions for the visiting partygoers.

The locals, called Geordies, are also honest. Mate John and I decided one evening to take a visit to Quayside, which was a bit of a novelty for us. You might recall that in the early days of mobile phones they were much bigger than they became later, although that trend seems to be reversing now. We were issued with a kind of holster that housed the phone and it would be threaded onto your belt. The problem with them was that because of their weight, if you took your trousers off to sit on a toilet seat, they would fall off the belt. That happened to me during our Quayside visit but, being full of grog, I did not notice until I woke up the next morning. I was issued with a new phone, but felt guilty enough about the loss to revisit the waterfront and try to find the old one. After walking up and down for a while, I saw a pub which looked vaguely familiar and went in to enquire if anyone had handed a phone in. To my astonishment, the barman produced my old one. Whoever found it had not even made a two-hour call to some overseas friend.

Well, the Geordies might be honest, but they are just as ridiculous as everyone else in the UK about soccer, which they insist on calling football. There are numerous levels of competition, but the two most important ones are the Premier League (similar to Australia's Rugby League and Aussie Rules competitions) and the FA Cup, which is a knockout competition with hundreds of competitors where theoretically at least, a third-grade team can win the Cup.

Sometime in August, an FA Cup game was scheduled between Newcastle, a first-grade team, and nearby Sunderland, which played in a lower grade. There had apparently been an ongoing grudge between these two teams for decades so a fierce match was anticipated. One of the Junior Clerks from the FMD office we worked from arranged for a bunch of us to attend with him. What a revelation! Our mild-mannered clerk turned into a screaming, raging bigot, amazing me with not only his vehemence, but also his easy command of the full spectrum of expletives. There were many memorable insults delivered, but the one that sticks most firmly in my mind was his description of a Sunderland player (or was it the referee?) as a 'fucking slap-headed tosser!' Equanimity was finally restored when Newcastle won in extra time.

Newcastle sits on the River Tyne and as I said earlier, it is very beautiful, particularly in the late afternoon. On a number of occasions, we drove out along the valley and had dinner in pubs in various small towns or villages. Hadrian's

Wall, which was built either to keep out the wild Scots or to delineate the furthest extent of the Roman Empire, depending on whom you believe, was nearby much of the time as we headed west. It must be said that it was responsible for some pretty unimaginative nomenclature in the region. One night we had dinner in Hadrian's Hotel in the village of Walls! There were several forts along the wall and remnants of some of them survive. The most notable is Vindolanda where, in the late 20th century, a pile of documents written on very thin wooden tablets was unearthed. These included the first example of a woman writing in Latin ever recorded. The wife of a Roman officer, she was inviting her friend to her birthday party.

Working for FMD eradication was a great experience. There had been many instances of confrontation and heartbreak early on in the outbreak, as people's life works were destroyed when whole herds had to be killed, but, luckily for me, most of that was past by the time I arrived. Most of what I did was easy and pleasant and property owners were surprisingly agreeable.

Where an area was designated 'suspect', every property had to be visited to see what cloven-hoofed animals, if any, resided there. If animals were found, the property would be visited by another team to test the herd or flock. My job was to be one of the people driving around the countryside checking each farm for livestock. The exceptional accuracy and detail of the British ordinance survey maps made this fairly simple. The only problem was, being used to the distances in Australia, I was inclined to overshoot boundaries, expecting paddocks to be bigger. Quite often though, we (we usually worked in teams of two) would finish by, say, 3pm and headquarters would tell us to go home and they would call us if necessary. It only happened once. Being finished at 3pm in England in the summer meant it was probably six hours till nightfall, so there were often opportunities to play tourist.

One day when working alone, and almost finished, I came across a massive castle, Bamburgh Castle, of which I had never heard, on a cliff overlooking the sea. I parked and went in and was amazed. That happened a lot to me in Britain. Apparently, it had been a good spot to use as a fort since prehistoric times and was recorded as having been taken over by Ida the Flame Bearer in 538 AD. It also turned out that Bamburgh was the town where Grace Darling rowed out to sea in a dreadful storm to rescue a bunch of people from a sinking ship. I suspect I might have been the only person for 100 miles who didn't know that.

The area I was in at the time is north of Newcastle and also incorporated Alnwick Castle, of Harry Potter fame—the one with lion statues that have straight, skinny tails. I am familiar with the pronunciation of 'wick' in England.

Mostly. Warwick and Berwick drop the 'w', so I was pretty confident in asking a local how to get to the town of Alnwick, which I pronounced 'Aln-ick'. Ha ha! Annick! Not only was I corrected, but the corrector was a friend of one of the women who worked in the administration centre I went to every morning in Newcastle. The following day when I turned up for work, I was greeted by calls of 'Went to Alnick yesterday, did you?' Ha! Great glee! Wait! It's not over. There is another town, south-west of Durham, called Hunwick. I was not too sure how to get there, so stopped the car beside a bloke walking along the road and said, 'Can you tell me where the turnoff is to Hunnick?' He said, 'Eh?' So, I repeated the question. He sneered down his nose at me, as only a certain type of Pommie can, and said, 'You mean Hun-wick?' Fuck me! I think they do it on purpose.

When Flora and I had lived in Bedford, we ate salmon once a week. We thought it was beautiful, but were regularly told that it was farmed salmon and not a patch on the wild-caught fish. So, when I finished with the FMD job, I hired a car and took a trip around Scotland, firstly to have a good look at the place and, secondly, to find a meal of wild salmon. Could not be done. I don't know what happens to all of the wild fish that are caught, but it was nowhere near any restaurant I went to and, it seems to me, never had been. The drive was well worth it though, particularly the amazingly spectacular north-west coast.

I had not been sure what I might do to keep body and soul together when I got back to Australia, but had got a suggestion from an Iraqi vet, Omar, who was now a naturalised Australian working in the meat inspection field. He had taken some time off from his job in Victoria and suggested I might contact the Business Manager for that state with a view to getting work as a contract vet in the Australian Quarantine and Inspection Service (AQIS). That seemed like a good idea, so when I took a break in July and came home for a couple of weeks, I rang the Victorian Manager. He was totally unimpressed and gave me no encouragement whatsoever. I think he thought I wanted a full-time job. Anyhow, I took the opportunity of calling the Queensland Government equivalent at the same time and he was very keen for me to work for him, so that solved that. When I got back to Newcastle, I ran across Omar and he asked me how I had got on. I explained that the Victorian had been totally uncooperative. In the workplace filled with vets of many different nationalities, I think Omar might have temporarily forgotten that I was an Aussie, because he replied, 'Oh, I wouldn't worry too much about him. He's what we call in Australia, a bit of a dickhead!'

* * *

HOME AGAIN

I got back to Oz in late September 2001 and, with the prospect of getting plenty of casual AQIS abattoir work, despite it being quite boring and/or unpleasant, life looked fairly settled. So, I bought a small farm on the Darling Downs, near Toowoomba. There was quite a good style wooden house, albeit it was in a fairly sad state, so Flora and I got it straightened up and tidied then rented it to a couple of excellent tenants. I also installed a centre pivot irrigation system to take advantage of the irrigation licence that was attached to the farm. Things looked quite good and the farm was in two blocks, so I decided to move a house onto the second one. I had done that before when we had the dairy farm and it had been a very positive move. Boy, oh boy! How things can change in twenty years in the world of bureaucracy. The earlier move had involved a bare minimum of interference and when it was completed, I phoned the Shire Clerk and asked if the Council would want to inspect the house and give it some sort of official seal of approval. He asked if we were living in it yet and I told him that we were. He then said, 'Well, it must be all right.' The final suggestion was that the Health Inspector might call in one day on his way home from work, but he never did.

Fast forward twenty years and I bought a removal house in Toowoomba. The first interference occurred when the Council decreed that they must inspect the house to see if it met their standards for removal. Fortunately, it did. I had already bought the house, so I cannot imagine what I could have done if it was decided that it could not be shifted. Burn it down?

The next exercise in stupidity gets the gold medal though. Like a lot of houses of its vintage, my new one had a stove nook in the kitchen where the wood stove was sited. I had originally thought to preserve the nook, but on reflection decided it would be more trouble than it was worth. The alternative was to put a big window into much of the space. The removalist/builder found a big, sliding glass window at a second-hand shop and it seemed ideal. But ... when the time came for the completed exercise to be inspected by the Council Officer, it emerged that the glass was the wrong thickness. A thickness of 2mm was not considered enough to protect inhabitants from the risk of flying glass in the event that someone spilt boiling fat on the window and it shattered. I am not making this up! We were supposed to have 3mm. Fortunately, the builder still had the receipt from when he had bought the window and it pre-dated the regulation change that required thicker glass, so we were allowed to keep the extremely dangerous window. To date nobody has been injured, as far as I know.

It isn't finished yet. Apparently, it was decided by the Council bureaucrats that I was not competent to manage my own comfort. They told me that I had to install insulation batts in the ceiling. I would have done that, but resented compulsion, and it gets better. I was also told that, because of the particular climate where the farm was, I needed a particular grade of batts. Up until that time I was not aware that they came in different sizes. Neither was the builder and they had already been installed. I told him what grade was needed and he said, 'Yes. That's what I got.' He was probably lying, but I didn't care.

There were a couple of other examples of bureaucratic interference, but after the window episode they barely rate a mention.

In 2007, I decided to sell the farm. A neighbouring horse spelling property had changed hands and the new owner was expanding the business and required more land. My irrigation setup was also a big attraction. He would have been quite happy to not have the removal house, but I think it might have helped him borrow the purchase money as the banks seem to like a bit of regular rental income. As it turned out, there wasn't much of that. The first tenants had to be evicted for non-payment. The house was then let to a couple of lesbians. Nobody is too concerned about other people's sexual inclinations these days, but that did not stop the next-door workers from referring to the rental house as the liquor barn! Same pronunciation, different spelling I suppose.

Selling the farm resulted in a nice profit, which was pretty unusual for most of my enterprises, so I worried about having to pay capital gains tax. I called the Taxation Department and was delighted to discover that when Peter Costello was Federal Treasurer, he had made the decision that for people in business, the profit from the sale of that business was equivalent to their superannuation, so the first $600,000 was not subject to tax. What a beauty! I had mentally been allocating a significant amount to pay the tax and now it was not needed, so I did what any intelligent person would do: squandered it on a six-month overseas trip.

In preparation for the journey, and in anticipation of doing lots of walking, I bought a pair of quite flash walking boots. As it turned out, they weren't all that flash as when we were walking across northern England along Hadrian's

Wall, the boots started to leak. That was a bit disappointing, so when we got to Edinburgh, where we were due to do a 'house sit' during the Fringe Festival, I contacted the American manufacturers. A very helpful lady there suggested I might get in touch with their British agents, which I did. The outcome was that I got back to the American and explained that the person I had spoken to was like a few Pommies I had run across and would rather have root canal fillings without anaesthetic than actually try to do something useful. Two days later the Yank lady contacted me again and told me to go to a certain Edinburgh shoe shop and get a free new pair. Which I did. I was interested to find that, although my new boots were actually better than my original ones, adjusted for the exchange rate, they probably only cost about two-thirds as much. I think we are getting ripped off in Oz.

Our six-month trip was a lot of fun and the final destination was India. We flew to Chennai (formerly Madras) and met up with a couple of friends, then took a van and driver on a tour of the south. The compulsory Kerala backwaters barge trip was well worthwhile and we had a very interesting drinking experience in one of the restaurants in Cochin. In this particular locality, I think because of proximity to a mosque or something, alcohol was forbidden. That did not stop it from being served though; the beer came 'disguised' in teapots. Four of us sat around our table with a china teapot each, along with a china cup each, and drank our beer, which I am quite sure would not have fooled a single person. And because the china was room temperature, the beer soon was as well!

India is an amazing place. I have no idea what the unemployment rate is, or even if it is estimated, but they seem to have the knack of making a job one person could do into several individual tasks requiring a different person for each one. Flora and her mate, Jill, went into a fabric shop and the counter formed a u-shape around three walls. The total length of the counter was probably 15m and there were fifteen people serving behind it! The other system that amazed us was in a tea museum we visited. As we exited, we passed through a shop and decided to buy some tea. First you select your tea and hand it to the man behind the counter. He then gives it to one of the girls to take to someone else to wrap it up. Another brings the package back to the first man who then gives it to us after we have gone through a similar procedure to pay for it.

Another fascinating example of job generation occurs on the train to the hill station of Ooty, which was where the British administrators used to go to avoid the oppressive heat of the Indian summer in Chennai. The train is a small, narrow-gauged one with three carriages and, as the track is quite steep, it travels at a very sedate pace. Before starting off, the security of the passengers must be confirmed by an official, one for each carriage, who stands at the open door and waves a flag. Later, when the train is underway, there are two occasions when there is a curve in the track and it is not possible to see more than 70 or 80m ahead. In both of these situations there is a man beside the track whose job it is to indicate whether or not it is safe to continue. I assume the possible perils include dead elephants on the track and bandits, but as the top speed of the train never exceeds about 15km/h, I really think the driver could stop in time to avoid disasters.

The last place we stayed before returning to Chennai to catch the plane home was Mysore. Coincidentally, the Maharaja's Cup meeting was on at the Mysore races while we were there, so mate Boyce and I decided to go. It was a pretty interesting experience. The horses were not as good as our Aussie thoroughbreds, but were all very well prepared and the track was excellent. It appeared that a local doctor had a large stable and his horses raced well. When it came Cup time, the doctor's entry was a long odds-on favourite, so not worth backing. However, I discovered that, in India, you can back a horse to run second, so that's what I did, having chosen an animal at a very long price. Just before the race was due to start though, the favourite was kicked by another horse and had to be withdrawn. Away they went and my animal looked to be travelling okay, so I was on good terms with myself when I saw it moving into third position as the field entered the straight. Shortly after, he got the better of the horse that had been running second and when he passed the furlong post I started shrieking with excitement. My glee was short-lived, sadly, as in the shadows of the winning post, the leader got a terrible stitch and practically stopped. My horse passed him! It was the only time in my life I was able to come home from the races and say that I would have picked up a small fortune but my useless bloody horse won!

* * *

We got back to Australia in the spring and started looking around for something to do. Brisbane suburbia was losing its appeal. Traffic was getting noticeably worse and barking dogs have always driven me mad, so we ended up on a lychee orchard at Goomboorian. If you are one of those people who say, 'Where in the bloody hell is Goomboorian?' you are not alone, because that is what I also said when I saw the listing. However, despite its obscurity, Goomboorian has a bit going for it, and not just the quality of its new residents. It is 30 minutes by car from Tin Can Bay, 45 minutes from Rainbow Beach and an easy hour's drive from Noosa. Frosts are rare, annual rainfall is 1250mm and on hot summer days, the Double Island 'Doctor' can be relied on to cool things off in the afternoon.

We have a great range of wildlife here, including kangaroos and wallabies which frequently hop through the garden, and the occasional koala visits, though they generally only stay a day. I have identified 54 species of birds and there are still some that remain a mystery to me. Dollar birds perform acrobatics when they come here to mate in the spring; a flock of exquisite Scarlet Honeyeaters arrived to feast on the Paper Bark flowers one year and have never returned, no matter how much I wish they would; and Noisy Friarbirds have us in stitches when they come to the Grevillea in our front garden for some nectar and stop feasting occasionally to have a prolonged gossip. We also have a couple of Flowering Ash trees which are a problem because every seed they drop seems to want to germinate and grow but as they attract the King Parrots and their close friends, perhaps the world's most beautiful birds, the Red-winged Parrots, they are forgiven.

We also seem to have got the knack of growing lychees at last so, while we have put the place on the market, I don't care if it does not sell for a while. I reckon I might be quite negotiable in a few years when I have become a crippled, dribbling vegetable, but not yet.

Things are still pretty good.

www.ingramcontent.com/pod-product-compliance
Lightning Source LLC
Chambersburg PA
CBHW021145080526
44588CB00008B/230
* 9 7 8 1 9 2 5 7 0 7 6 7 0 *